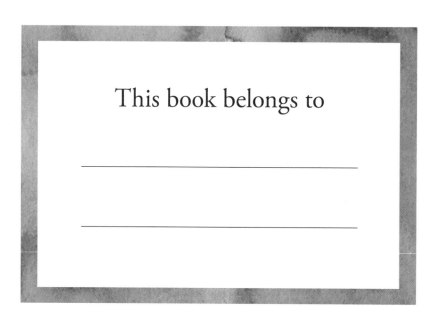

This book belongs to

_____

_____

BOOK *of*
CATHOLIC SIGNS & SYMBOLS

AN ILLUSTRATED GUIDE TO THEIR HISTORY AND MEANING

AMY WELBORN

LOYOLA PRESS.
A JESUIT MINISTRY
Chicago

MORE FROM LOYOLA KIDS

LOYOLA KIDS BOOK OF BIBLE STORIES
BY AMY WELBORN

LOYOLA KIDS BOOK OF HEROES
BY AMY WELBORN

LOYOLA KIDS BOOK OF SAINTS
BY AMY WELBORN

LOYOLA KIDS BOOK OF EVERYDAY PRAYERS
BY CATHERINE ODELL
AND MARGARET SAVITSKAS

LOYOLA PRESS.
A JESUIT MINISTRY

3441 N. Ashland Avenue
Chicago, Illinois 60657
(800) 621-1008
www.loyolapress.com

Cover and interior illustrations: Marina Seoane
Author photo: Jill Anders

ISBN-13: 978-0-8294-4651-7
Library of Congress Control Number: 2018938538

Printed in the United States of America
18 19 20 21 22 23 24 25 26 27 28 Versa 10 9 8 7 6 5 4 3 2 1

LOYOLA KIDS

BOOK *of*

CATHOLIC SIGNS & SYMBOLS

AN ILLUSTRATED GUIDE TO THEIR HISTORY AND MEANING

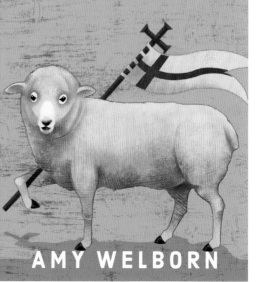

AMY WELBORN

Contents

God

Nativity of Jesus

Passion and Resurrection of Jesus

Passion and Resurrection *(continued)*

Mary

Saints

Contents *(continued)*

Old Testament: Story of God's People

In Church

In Church *(continued)*

At Home

In the Sacraments

Introduction

The Kingdom of Heaven is like…

   a mustard seed.

   a treasure hidden in a field.

Think about the most important things in your life: feelings, ideas, emotions, relationships, and hopes. Now try to explain these things in a way that communicates the depth and breadth and truth of what you've experienced.

It's hard. It might even be impossible. No matter how eloquent we are, what we express only touches the surface of what's real. What's more, the deeper and more important the reality, the more challenging it is to express with any accuracy.

But we still try, because we are created to do so. We're created in God's image, which means we're created to be in communion with God and others, to understand, to imagine, to love, and to create. To do so, we depend on metaphors and similes, signs and symbols.

Just as Jesus used that most absorbing means of human communication—the story—to communicate with us, he also used signs and symbolic language. The Scriptures are woven with imagery that remains fundamental to our understanding of God: rock, shepherd, right hand, and so on.

Spirituality involves the deepest realities of all: the human soul and its relation to the Creator. Signs and symbols play an especially rich and important role in this part of life.

It's important to understand the difference between a sign and a symbol. Signs and symbols are closely related but have slightly different meanings. Both stand for something else, but a sign does so in a simpler, more direct way. Words are signs, for example. Letters arranged in a certain way are a sign for the word and idea of "love." A symbol is more complex, less direct, and more open to different interpretations: a heart is a symbol for love.

Signs and symbols have always been important in Christian life and faith. Human beings are natural artists and communicators, so we use symbols to express complex realities. Early Christianity developed in an environment in which persecution was frequently a fact of life, so symbols became a way to communicate and build bonds and pass on the truths of the faith in ways that hostile outsiders could not understand.

Signs and symbols have played a vital role in Christian life over the centuries for another reason: for much of Christian history, most Christians could not read. In these pre-literate societies, most people learned about their faith orally as parents, catechists, and clergy passed on prayers and basic teachings. They also learned about their faith in cultures that used symbolic language and actions to express and make spiritual realities visible throughout the year. They lived in the rhythm of liturgical feasts and seasons. They participated in the Mass and other community prayers, rich with symbolic gestures, images, and even structured in a highly symbolic way from beginning to end. Their places of worship, great and small, were built on symbolic lines and bore symbolic artwork inside and out.

These people might not have been able to read, but they could *read*. Their books were made of stone, paint, tapestry threads, gestures, chant, and the seasons of the year. They could read this symbolic language of the faith. Their language was one that communicated the realities of salvation history and God's mercy and love through images of animals, plants, shapes, and design. They knew through these symbols that God is justice and beauty. They understood that with God they enjoyed the feast of the Eucharist or of a celebratory holy day.

We still speak this symbolic language, but the welcome increase in reading literacy and the importance we have given the written word have made it seem at times that what we can read on a printed page is somehow more real, more expressive of what is true. Because educated people have historically been considered superior to the uneducated, we tend to think that acquiring information through written words is more sophisticated, more mature than acquiring it through images, just as we consider that a sign of growing maturity in children is their ability to read books that have no pictures.

Yet, although the most profound realities of life—joy, love, passion, grief, hope—can certainly be expressed with words, how often do we raise our hands in resignation, knowing that in this moment, we've said all we can, even though we *know* and *mean* so much more? So often, there are no words.

The world of Christian signs and symbols is a gift for children. The simplicity of imagery meets them where they are, and the depth and richness of this same imagery prepares the soil for deeper understanding. When a child's faith is lived in a wealth of imagery at home, at church, and in broader culture, she is continually assured that she is not alone, that God is present in every aspect of this world he created, and that God meets her where she is. She's taught from the beginning that the world is much more than what we can initially apprehend. She's taught that the spiritual life involves soul and body, reason and imagination, ideas and the tangible. She learns to live faith in a biblical, holistic, Catholic way.

How to Use This Book

Use this book, first of all, as a beginning. What we offer here is just a small portion of the wealth of imagery that has evolved over two thousand years of Catholic culture and faith in every corner of the globe. The images and explanations you find here are the most common and well-known, but there are countless others not covered, some probably in your own church or home.

This book is designed to be used for young children or for older groups, including adults who want to know more about Catholic signs and symbols. The left-hand page for each sign/symbol provides a picture and a short, simple explanation to use with young children. Older readers can go to the right-hand page, "A Closer Look," which offers more detail.

Use *Loyola Kids Book of Catholic Signs & Symbols* as a reference for questions that arise when reading Scripture or visiting churches. Use it to inspire further exploration. The discovery that a lily is a symbol for the Blessed Virgin or that a circle and a triangle both symbolize God can lead children and those who teach them to notice more details in the images they encounter in books, homes, and churches.

Use this book to help your children grow in their understanding of faith and deepen their connection with God and his saints.

- Spend time in your church before or after Mass to study the imagery there: windows, paintings, statues, and even furnishings and the shape of the building. Explore the imagery you find in other churches as well, near your home or on your travels. How are symbols and images the same or different among churches?

- Ask older Catholic relatives and acquaintances about the images they remember from childhood, especially those they treasured, such as pictures of saints or fonts with holy water.

- Visit a Catholic bookstore or gift shop and find images and objects to put in your home, including a child's room.

- Go to museums! Sometimes we are hesitant to take children to museums, but if the visit is structured with a child's limitations and needs in mind, it can be very rewarding. For the purposes of exploring Christian signs and symbols, get acquainted with the museum's collection online and plan your visit, which can be as short or long as you need. Medieval and Renaissance collections can reinforce and enrich the images you find in this book. Make a game of it: How are the various images of Madonna and Child the same or different? Can they guess the saint in a painting because of objects that appear in the picture? *Can you?*

For pastors, directors of religious education, principals, and coordinators: help children engage with God through signs and symbols by providing an environment rich with them. Help children *read* and enter the faith in a deeper way through the images they see on the walls and through what you share with them in the form of holy cards and other sacramentals.

We know God loves us, and we know that God's love is more than we can capture with even the most exact words or detailed images. Our human notions of love are limited because of our weakness and because all we can really describe is what we now see "through a glass darkly" on earth. So images, signs, and symbols help. They help us dig deeper, they help bring us into more profound communion with the Lord, and from the very beginning, these powerful signs and symbols lead our children on that journey to love beyond words, as well.

GOD

Like a shepherd he feeds his flock;
in his arms he gathers the lambs.

Isaiah 40:11

H ow can we describe our great, loving God who is so far above us and yet so near? Signs and symbols help, but what they express offers just a glimpse of who God is.

What symbols tell us about God is true and real, but they are only a beginning. They hint of what is to come by helping us focus on what we can see and touch right now. They are an invitation to come closer, to listen, and to enter communion with the God who loves us.

Circles and Triangles

God created the whole universe, from the tiniest atom to the great, swirling galaxies. God is beyond us, but God is with us too. Shapes show us mysterious truths about God. A circle has no beginning or end, reminding us that God has no beginning or end—God is eternal. A triangle shows how one thing can have three sides. There is only one God, but he meets us as Father, Son, and Holy Spirit. A circle and a triangle drawn together are a symbol of the Trinity: Three Persons in one God.

A Closer Look . . .

n artist reveals some of her personality in what she creates: painting, sculpture, music, or writing.

God is the greatest artist and creator of all, and God's creation reveals to us God the artist's nature. God is beauty, reason, and order. God is all-powerful and all-knowing. God is one.

Because God loves us so much, he tells us even more about himself than what we can conclude from reason or nature. He reveals the great mystery of God as Trinity: God is Three Persons—Father, Son, and Holy Spirit—in one God.

God builds shapes right into creation. We see all kinds of shapes around us: bubbles, spheres, and mountain peaks reaching to the sky. They help us think more about what God has revealed about himself, and so people have tried to understand God by using shapes to describe what God is like.

A **circle** is a shape with no beginning or end, like God, who is one and eternal.

A **triangle** can have three equal sides. Father, Son, and Spirit are all equally God.

A **trefoil** joins three circles in a way that forms a triangle. A **triqueta** meshes the shapes of a circle and triangle so that there's a triangle at the center and all the arcs are of equal size. These symbols bring together circles and triangles to help us enter the great mystery of the Trinity: Three Divine Persons in One God.

Hand

God is pure spirit and does not have a physical body. But you and I do. For instance, we have hands, and we use them in so many ways. With our hands we can make things or express how we feel. A picture that shows God's hand coming out of a cloud helps us understand that God is right here in the world with us and that he is busy doing things too.

n image of a human hand can represent how God is present in our world. In the Bible, God's mighty hand protects and saves God's people from danger (Exodus 3:19–20). In scenes of creation, Jesus' baptism, or his crucifixion, you can sometimes see a hand emerging from a cloud above. That's a way of showing that God is present and active and rules over all these mysteries.

In the ancient world, right and left had special meanings. If you were at someone's right hand, you shared that person's power and blessing. The Bible describes Jesus as sitting at the right hand of the Father, and Jesus describes the Last Judgment as a time when the righteous will be set apart on his right hand (Matthew 25:31–46).

Often, in depictions of Jesus, his right hand—and always his right hand—is raised in blessing, even if he's being depicted as a baby! Sometimes he has two fingers raised together with the thumb and the other two folded down and meeting. This symbolizes the Trinity as well as Jesus' divine and human natures.

In other images, Jesus' fingers are arranged so that they symbolize the Greek letters ICXC, which are the first and last letters of the words Jesus Christ in Greek.

Shepherd

A shepherd cares for sheep, helping them find food and water. He protects them from harm. That's what God does: he cares for us as a shepherd cares for a flock of sheep. Jesus tells us that he is the Good Shepherd. He knows us, and we know him. If we're lost, Jesus will find us so we can be safe with him again. From early times, Christians showed Jesus as a shepherd caring for us, his sheep.

A Closer Look . . .

S ince Old Testament times, God's people have used the shepherd image to represent God. They prayed, "The Lord is my shepherd" from Psalm 23. When Jesus was growing up and receiving his religious training, he probably memorized that psalm. It's no surprise that later, in his public ministry, he used stories about shepherds and sheep.

Shepherds and their flocks were a common sight for the Israelites. They understood that sheep depended on a shepherd to lead and protect them. And a good shepherd knew each of his sheep and was committed to the flock's welfare, sometimes fighting wolves and other predators to protect the sheep.

God, like a shepherd, keeps us safe and protects us from danger. He guides us to where we need to be for a rich, full life. Jesus calls himself our shepherd. He goes further in John 10 to say that he is the Good Shepherd who knows each of us personally and who is willing to lay down his life for us. Jesus also reminds us that if even one sheep wanders from the rest of the flock, the shepherd will go find it and bring it back (Luke 15:3–7).

The shepherd was a common image in many cultures, often used in gardens. Some of the earliest Christian uses of the shepherd image appeared on or around tombs and are in certain catacombs in Rome.

Lamb

When God freed the Israelites from slavery in Egypt, the blood of a lamb painted over their doors saved their lives. People sacrificed lambs in temple worship to show their repentance. Jesus is the Lamb of God because he offered his life as a sacrifice for our sins. Sometimes in art, the Lamb of God is shown as a sacrifice on an altar. Sometimes the lamb stands and holds a flag, to show that he is conquering sin.

A Closer Look . . .

The night that God freed his people from slavery in Egypt, he told them that if they painted the blood of a lamb over their doorways, death would pass over their homes. Because of the blood of the lamb, they were saved on that first Passover.

Lambs were important in worship, too. The ancient Israelites offered all sorts of crops and animals in sacrifice as a way of thanking God and showing sorrow for sin. A young lamb was one of the finest sacrifices they could offer.

So, when John the Baptist saw Jesus and said, "Behold the Lamb of God," his listeners understood. They also might have remembered the words of the prophet Isaiah, who described a Suffering Servant who would, out of love and obedience, accept suffering and be led to slaughter like a lamb.

Agnus Dei is Latin for "lamb of God." We see Jesus as the Lamb of God depicted primarily in two ways. The lamb might be lying on an altar, as in a sacrifice. Or the lamb is standing, holding a white flag with a cross on it, triumphant over sin and death. In either of these you might see other symbols: the lamb's breast might be pierced with blood pouring from it, or there might be water flowing around it, expressing a vision of the Lamb from the Book of Revelation: "a river of life-giving water, sparkling like crystal, flowing from the throne of God and of the Lamb" (Revelation 22:1).

Fish

L ong ago, Christians noticed that the letters in the Greek word for "fish"—*Ichthys*—could be a sort of puzzle that showed them Jesus. The letters of that word were also the first letters of the Greek words "Jesus Christ, the Son of God, Savior." Early Christians drew this symbol as a sign of their faith, especially in times when they had to keep their beliefs secret from Roman authorities.

A Closer Look . . .

T he early Christians had given their lives to Jesus. They decorated their worship places and tombs with signs of this identity. One of the most important of these early signs was a fish.

In the Gospels, Jesus multiplies loaves and fishes to feed multitudes. After the Resurrection, Jesus appears to his disciples on a beach at the Sea of Galilee, grilling fish for their breakfast. Fish are a sign of Jesus' care for us and a symbol of how he feeds us with his very life in the Eucharist.

But there's another reason the early Christians liked this sign. It was more than just a sign to others of who they were. It was a symbol that helped them remember something important about Jesus. Most of these early Christians spoke Greek, and the Greek word for "fish" is Ichthys. Each of the letters in this word is a first letter of a word in the phrase: Iesous Christos Theou Yios Soter: "Jesus Christ, the Son of God, Savior."

We're baptized, and we bear the name of Christ—Christian— and his life of grace within us. An ancient Christian writer named Tertullian put it this way: we're like little fishes, born in the waters of Baptism, and to remain safe and spiritually healthy, we must stay in the water with him: Ichthys.

Christogram

F rom the earliest days, Christians have used letters as symbols to stand for Jesus. *Chi* and *rho* are the first two letters of the word *Christ* in Greek. *IHS* are the first three letters of *Jesus* in Greek. *Alpha* and *Omega* are the first and last letters of the Greek alphabet. In the Book of Revelation, Jesus describes himself as the Alpha and the Omega, the Lord who is with us always, from the beginning to the end.

A Closer Look . . .

 e don't always have the time or space to write out our full names or other words. Think of all the abbreviations and acronyms we use every day: TGIF — ID — RSVP — LOL.

The earliest Christians abbreviated Jesus' name. Over time, the arrangements of these letters became symbols. These early believers spoke mostly Greek, so the main symbolic abbreviations that have come down to us today are rooted in Greek.

Chi-Rho are the first two letters of the word **Christos**, or **Christ**, which means "anointed one."

I-H-S are the first three letters of **IHSUS**, the name of Jesus in Greek.

Alpha and **Omega** are the first and last letters of the Greek alphabet. In the Book of Revelation, Jesus says, "I am the Alpha and the Omega, the one who is and who was and who is to come, the almighty" (Revelation 22:13). Through this, we learn that Jesus is fully God, present everywhere and from eternity.

We see these letters in many places: on Bible and lectionary covers, on altar coverings and carved in ambos. We see them on the paschal candle. These letters in an ancient language speak to us today in the same way they spoke to the earliest Christians, revealing to us that Jesus is Lord, always and forever.

Sacred Heart

We think of our heart as the place love comes from. God is love, and so the human heart of Jesus symbolizes the love that God has for us. Every part of the image of the Sacred Heart of Jesus expresses this love. It is pierced by the wounds of the Crucifixion. It is surrounded by thorns that remind us how he suffered for us. And it burns with flames of love.

A Closer Look . . .

*M*y heart is bursting with love. . . . My heart is broken. . . . "Were not our hearts burning within us?"

Science classes teach us that our hearts pump blood, the source of life, through our bodies. But many cultures have understood the heart also as the core of a person and the source of love. One of the basic laws of the Jewish people commands them to love the Lord with their whole hearts.

It makes sense that the symbol of Jesus' Sacred Heart helps us understand the great love Jesus has for us.

When we see Jesus' Sacred Heart, sometimes it is pictured apart from Jesus' body, and sometimes it is superimposed on his chest, and he is pointing to it. There are some variations in how the Sacred Heart is presented, but usually you will see some common symbols. The heart is pierced, and perhaps there are drops of blood. This helps us remember how Jesus' side was pierced when he was on the Cross. Thorns, a symbol of our sin and Jesus' suffering, surround the heart. The flames coming out of the Sacred Heart help us remember that Jesus' love burns with intensity.

The devotion to the Sacred Heart is ancient but was made more popular by Saint Margaret Mary Alacoque, a seventeenth-century French nun. She experienced visions of Jesus asking her to spread the Good News about his love by encouraging others to contemplate his Sacred Heart.

Dove

R ight before Jesus began preaching and teaching, his cousin
John the Baptist baptized Jesus in the Jordan River. When
Jesus came up out of the water, God sent a sign from heaven:
a dove. That's why a dove is a symbol of the Holy Spirit. Jesus
promised that the Holy Spirit would come to us and be God's
presence with us every day.

A Closer Look . . .

The Holy Trinity is at the heart of our faith; we begin all of our prayer in the name of the Trinity, and we've been baptized in that name. But Christians have always been careful expressing this truth with symbols. We want to remember that while symbols help us come closer to God, our ideas, words, and drawings only give us hints of what God is like.

In the Old Testament story of Noah and the great Flood, Noah and his family know that they can finally leave the ark when the dove Noah sent out returns with an olive sprig in its beak. This is proof that plants are growing again and there is dry land on which people can live. The catastrophe is over, and humans have a second chance on earth. Historically, a dove with an olive branch has represented peace; nations and governments have used this symbol.

In the New Testament, we see the dove again. When Jesus is baptized by John in the Jordan River, the Holy Spirit descends on Jesus in the form of a dove. Thus, the dove becomes the Christian symbol for the Holy Spirit, God's presence among us, promised by Jesus.

A dove does not appear in the Scripture story of the Annunciation, when the angel told Mary that, by the power of the Holy Spirit, she would have a baby whom people would come to know as the Messiah. But we sometimes see a dove in pictures of that conversation.

We know that the Holy Spirit brings many gifts—seven, traditionally—and that there are many fruits to allowing the Holy Spirit to flourish in our lives.

Fire

A fter Jesus ascended into heaven, the Apostles wanted to obey his command to go out to the whole world and spread the Good News, but they were afraid. They were so afraid that when they gathered in Jerusalem to pray, they locked the door. Through that locked door and strong walls, the gift that Jesus had promised—the *Paraclete*, the helper—arrived. After a mighty wind filled the room, tongues of fire appeared over each of their heads. It was the Holy Spirit, bringing wisdom, courage, and many more gifts to the Apostles. They were no longer afraid!

A Closer Look . . .

Fire burns. We think of that burning as destructive and harmful, but that is not the whole story of fire.

Fire also warms us and helps us see. We cook with fire. Fire refines, purifies, and transforms substances. You can put what seems like an ordinary rock in fire, and then it comes out of the fire as a precious metal.

In the Bible, fire is a complicated symbol of God's presence among us. God appeared as a pillar of fire at night to lead the Israelites during the Exodus. God was present to Moses in the form of a burning bush.

The sacrifice of the first fruits of a harvest and the best animals was an important way that the ancient Israelites worshiped God. The burning fire of the sacrifice was a sign to the people that God had accepted their love and praise.

When we use the symbol of fire to describe God's presence, we're reminded that God's love is strong, intense, and powerful. It changes things.

At the Last Supper, Jesus had promised that he would send to the Apostles a helper, a **Paraclete**. That promise was fulfilled at Pentecost. The frightened Apostles had locked themselves in a room in Jerusalem and were praying when the Holy Spirit, as tongues of fire, alighted over each of their heads. It's the same Spirit who comes to us in Baptism and Confirmation: the Holy Spirit, God's energizing, burning presence in our hearts.

Clouds and Wind

The Bible tells us of many times when people experienced God through nature. God guided his people through the desert in the form of a cloud. God spoke to Moses from a cloud on Mount Sinai. Jesus ascended into a cloud and told his Apostles that when he returned, it would be on a cloud of glory. And at Pentecost, the Holy Spirit entered the Apostles' lives as a mighty, rushing wind.

A Closer Look . . .

od comes to us in many ways. He is present to us most importantly through the grace he offers through the Body of Christ on earth, the Church. We can also meet God in and through life in the world he made: in the quiet of our hearts and in acts of charity. We can even meet this mighty and mysterious God in what God has created.

The People of God often met him in clouds—clouds that hide and reveal, clouds that, like God, cannot be controlled by us. On the journey from Egypt to the Promised Land, God led the people in the form of a cloud by day. God spoke to Moses from a cloud on Mount Sinai, when he, the Lord, shared the gift of the Law.

We encounter Jesus as Lord through clouds, too. God's voice comes from a cloud at Jesus' baptism. Jesus enters a cloud when he is transfigured. He tells the Apostles that he will return to earth on a cloud of glory, and he ascends into the clouds of the heavens.

Before Jesus ascended, he promised that he would send a helper, a **Paraclete**. When the Holy Spirit came to the Apostles at Pentecost, it first entered their lives in that locked room as another powerful part of God's creation: a mighty, roaring wind.

NATIVITY OF JESUS

A shoot shall sprout from the stump of Jesse,
and from his roots a bud shall blossom.

Isaiah 11:1

M atthew and Luke tell us what happened when Jesus was born in Bethlehem. Their Gospels give us most of the signs and symbols that help us remember and celebrate Jesus' birth. Over the centuries, Christians added to the meaning of these symbols. They have also added symbols to help us understand and celebrate Christmas. All these, from oxen to angels to Jesse trees to Christmas trees, help us do more than celebrate a happy time. They help us think about why Jesus came among us and what he offers all the people of the world.

Nativity Scene

When we set up a Nativity scene or look at a painting of the baby Jesus, we see images that come from the Gospels of Matthew and Luke. Mary, Joseph, and the baby are surrounded by animals in a stable or cave. Luke tells us that shepherds come to adore Jesus, and Matthew tells about the wise men following the star to find Jesus. Angels announce the Good News. All are gathered around Jesus, and so are we!

A Closer Look . . .

 ngels, shepherds, and Magi. Animals. Mary and Joseph and the baby Jesus. We see Nativity scenes in churches, in our homes, and in paintings.

Most of the images in a Nativity scene come from the Gospels of Matthew and Luke, enriched by prayerful imagination and symbolism. Luke tells us that the newborn Jesus was laid in a manger, where animals feed. In Nativity scenes you will almost always see two specific creatures: an ox and an ass. This is inspired by Isaiah 1:3: "An ox knows its owner, and an ass, its master's manger." Christians have understood this image to reflect all creation's awareness of God's presence among us.

Artists weave into the Nativity scene symbols of the rest of Jesus' life and death. Light may come from the infant, who is the Light of the World. In some images, Jesus' manger resembles a tomb or coffin, reminding us that he suffered and died. A nearby lamb hints that this is the Lamb of God. Crumbling buildings in the landscape represent the old world that Jesus will renew. Once you start looking, you can see all sorts of signs that help you understand more about Jesus.

Saint Francis of Assisi used real animals and a feeding trough in a cave to create a Nativity scene in Greccio, Italy, in 1223. Since then, people from around the world have welcomed Jesus into their lives and cultures by imagining him as one of them, entering their own time and place—because that is exactly what he does.

Advent Wreath

I n the weeks before Christmas, an Advent wreath helps us prepare for Jesus' coming. Every week we light one of the candles that are symbols of Jesus, who is the Light of the World. The candles are arranged in a circle that reminds us that God has no beginning or end. The colors of the candles match the Advent-season colors. Three are violet, the color of penance, which is sorrow for our sins. One is pink or rose-colored to remind us that we look forward to the joy of celebrating Jesus' coming.

A Closer Look . . .

F or big celebrations such as Christmas, we spend a lot of time preparing. We cook, clean, plan, and practice. Because Christmas celebrates Jesus' birth, we prepare spiritually, too. Advent is the name of the four-week season of preparation for Christmas. We take quiet time to pray more and read the Bible. An Advent wreath can be part of this preparation at home and at the church.

Wreaths with candles were used in ancient pagan communities to signify hope for spring while in the middle of winter. During the Middle Ages, Christians integrated the lighted wreath into their preparations for Christmas. The four candles, which represented the four thousand years between Adam and Jesus, remind us that Jesus is the Light of the World. The candles are usually the Advent colors you see in church. The candles for weeks one, two, and four are violet, the color of penance. Week three is Gaudete Sunday—**Gaudete** means "rejoice," and its color is rose. On that Sunday, along with Mary, we are filled with joy because the Messiah is coming.

The Advent wreath is a circle, the shape that reminds us of God because it has no beginning or end. Some like to fashion Advent wreaths out of evergreen branches such as laurel or holly. The evergreen calls to mind the eternal life that Jesus brings us, and even the specific types have symbolic meaning: laurel was used as a prize in the ancient world and so represents Jesus' victory over suffering. Holly has pointy, sharp leaves and so reminds us of Jesus' humble sacrifice for us.

When using an Advent wreath at home, usually the family lights the appropriate candle(s) at dinnertime and uses Advent prayers and readings.

Christmas Tree

We use evergreen trees for Christmas trees because those trees don't lose their leaves in the autumn—they look green and alive all year long. This reminds us of God's never-ending love for us. When we gather around a Christmas tree, we can call it a tree of life. Sin and death entered the world when Adam and Eve ate forbidden fruit from a tree in the Garden of Eden. Then Jesus saved the world when he died on a cross—on wood from a tree.

A Closer Look . . .

If anything says "Christmas!" it's a tree. Whether it's a live tree or an artificial one, when we see an evergreen tree, we think of Christmas.

Trees have been important symbols in many religions, and from earliest times, evergreen trees have reminded people of life through winter and darkness. The evergreen tree has a specific meaning for Christians. Long ago, European Christians celebrated December 24 as the feast of Adam and Eve, our first parents. They put up a "Paradise Tree" decorated with fruit. It was a way of remembering how human beings had eaten fruit from the forbidden Tree of Knowledge of good and evil. That sadness was replaced by joy the next day, December 25, when they could celebrate Jesus, born to save us from that sin and open the way back to God. Jesus would demonstrate his love by dying on a cross, made from a tree. A Christmas tree is a tree of life!

This tradition developed over the centuries. In some cultures, people hung wafers from the tree's branches to remind them of the Eucharist. People put rows of lights on shelves at Christmas, and eventually they put these lights on the Christmas tree. The first Christmas lights were candles, and now we have strings of electric bulbs. These lights remind us of Jesus, who is the Light of the World.

And everywhere, we surround our Christmas trees with gifts: small gifts that echo the greatest gift of all: Jesus himself, who was born to us and lived among us. His love is evergreen, lasting through eternity.

Lights and Star

L ight is the first thing God created. It's a sign of his loving, creative power. Jesus tells us that he is the "light of the world." John writes in the beginning of his Gospel that Jesus brings light that darkness cannot overcome. At Christmas we decorate our houses with lights inside and out. We put lights on trees. We light special lanterns, and in the darkness, the flickering flames remind us how Jesus changes the world—and us.

A Closer Look . . .

God created a good, beautiful world, and he began by creating light (Genesis 1:1). But sin has darkened the world. Our own sin darkens our understanding and our ability to love. God wants us to live in the light, so he gave us his Son, Jesus, to be the world's Savior. The prophet Isaiah said of this Messiah, "Arise! Shine, for your light has come" (Isaiah 60:1).

John's Gospel does not include stories of Jesus' birth. Instead, at the beginning, John tells us other important things about Jesus. He is the Word of God made flesh, and he is the light that darkness cannot overcome (John 1:5). Later in John's Gospel, Jesus describes himself as the "light of the world" (John 8:12).

That's why lights are such an important part of Christmas. It begins with the star that led the Magi to Jesus, a star that's often represented symbolically with four points so that it looks like a cross. We celebrate this star and the light of Jesus by decorating our homes with all kinds of lights, inside and out. In Europe, people celebrate Christmas with bonfires in churchyards and town squares. In the Philippines, beautiful, colorful lanterns called **parols** are a part of Christmas. In the Ukraine, a Christmas candle is baked into a loaf of bread, a reminder that Jesus is the "light of the world" *and* the "bread of life." The light of Jesus conquers darkness everywhere in the world and in our own hearts, too.

Jesse Tree

Prophets such as Isaiah gave hope to God's people. They said that the Messiah would come from the "root of Jesse" and bring the world mercy and peace. Jesse was King David's father, and "root of Jesse" means that Jesus came from that family. A Jesse tree has branches that are decorated with symbols of the history of God's people. It reminds us that Jesus fulfilled God's promise—that he is the Messiah.

A Closer Look . . .

 avid was the greatest of Israel's kings. Anointed by God, he conquered Jerusalem, brought the ark of the covenant there, and composed many of the psalms. Later, the people of Israel stopped following God, and their nation declined in power. The people wanted salvation—they wanted to live again as God's people. The prophets told them that God would send them a Savior, a Messiah, who would make all things right.

One of these prophets, Isaiah, said that the Savior would also be from the "root of Jesse." Jesse was David's father. This meant that the Messiah would come from David's family. The Gospel writers Matthew and Luke both tell us that Jesus was, indeed, a descendant of David. Over the centuries, Christians put this truth into picture form by imagining a tree growing from a person: Jesse.

This image, which you find in stained glass, in books, or even carved into stone walls of churches, usually shows Jesse reclining with a tree growing from his side. On the branches are Jesus' ancestors or maybe the prophets. At the top of the tree we usually see Mary holding Jesus.

Today, we often make Jesse trees for our homes or classrooms during Advent. We might make them out of paper or cardboard or the branches of a real tree. Our Jesse trees are usually decorated with symbols of the history of God's people: Jacob's ladder, the tablet of the Ten Commandments, or David's harp. With each ornament, we remember and celebrate God's love for us, ever ancient and ever new.

Magi

M atthew's Gospel tells us of "wise men from the East" who
followed a star to the new King, Jesus, born in Bethlehem.
The word we use for wise men is *Magi*. Matthew doesn't tell
us how many Magi there were. We imagine that there were
three because they brought three gifts: gold, frankincense,
and myrrh. Since early times, Christians have called the three
wise men Caspar, Melchior, and Balthasar. We celebrate the
Magi and their gifts on the feast of the Epiphany, twelve days
after Christmas.

A Closer Look . . .

esus came to earth out of love for all people, and all people from everywhere on earth are invited to worship him. The Gospels tell us this from the beginning of Jesus' life. The first to arrive at the manger to see the infant Jesus were shepherds, who were poor outcasts. And then, according to Matthew's Gospel, wise men from the East arrived, Gentiles who were not even part of Israel.

These wise men, also called **Magi**, were priestly scholars who studied the universe for signs. In their wisdom, they had discovered a star that would lead them to a newly born king.

Matthew doesn't tell us how many Magi came to adore Jesus, and he doesn't name them. But he does tell us about their three kinds of gifts. The gift of gold reminds us that Jesus is king. The frankincense reminds us of Jesus' priestly role between human beings and God the Father. Myrrh was used to anoint the bodies of the dead, and so it reminds us of Jesus' sacrifice on the Cross. An early tradition in the Christian community gave names to the Magi: Caspar, Melchior, and Balthasar.

Were they kings? We don't know, but we think of them that way partly because of an ancient psalm we pray on Epiphany, the feast when we remember them:

"The western kings of Tarshish and other distant lands will bring him tribute. . . . All kings will bow before him, and all nations will serve him" (Psalm 72:10–11).

PASSION AND RESURRECTION OF JESUS

The soldiers wove a crown out of thorns and placed it on his head, and clothed him in a purple cloak.

John 19:2

J esus came into the world to heal our brokenness. Through his Death and Resurrection, he conquered sin and death. All four Gospels tell us of Jesus' Passion, and so most of the signs and symbols that help us understand this central mystery of our faith have origins in their witness.

As Christians reflected on these signs and symbols over the centuries, they made other connections as well. They remembered images from the Old Testament that helped them understand what Jesus had done. They saw patterns even in the rhythms of life around them. These ordinary aspects of life brought them closer to this great mystery: life and hope have sprung out of death, through God's power and love.

Cross and Crucifixion

J esus was the Son of God who came into the world to save us from sin and death. He preached, healed people, and demonstrated what true love does and says. And just as the prophets and Jesus predicted, he suffered. Religious authorities condemned him for blasphemy. Roman authorities accused him of rebellion, so he was executed under Roman law.

A Closer Look . . .

rucifixion was such a horrible punishment that it was not used on Roman citizens. The Romans reserved it for those who they thought were the worst criminals. The convicted carried part of the cross to the public place of execution. They were tied and nailed to the cross and left to die a long, painful death.

In images of the Crucifixion, we see Jesus on the cross on a hill outside Jerusalem's walls; it was called Golgotha, which means "place of the skull." We also call it Calvary, from the Latin **calva**, which means "bald head" or "skull." Most of Jesus' Apostles had run away, fearing that the Romans would arrest them, too. Depictions of the Crucifixion show Jesus' mother, Mary, usually wearing blue or black; Mary Magdalene wearing red; and the young disciple John. We see Roman soldiers and perhaps Jewish religious leaders looking on. Some of the soldiers are gambling for Jesus' garments. One is piercing his side with a lance; another offers him sour wine on a sponge. We might see onlookers who are mocking Jesus. On either side of Jesus, two criminals are being crucified.

All four Gospels tell us of Jesus' Crucifixion. Paintings, sculptures, and stained glass tell those Gospel stories without words, helping us be present with Jesus in prayerful sadness for his suffering and gratitude for his sacrifice.

Arma Christi:
Instruments of the Passion

J esus suffered and died on the Cross because he loves us. Jesus was accused of claiming to be a king, so soldiers put a crown of thorns on his head to make fun of him. Nails were used to put him on the Cross, and a soldier pierced Jesus' side with a spear. We remember Jesus' love when we see images of some of these objects of the Crucifixion.

A Closer Look . . .

Symbols help Christians draw close to Jesus. We know Jesus' love from his suffering and death, and symbols of his Passion help us focus on that love. We see these objects in art that depicts scenes of the Passion, but they are also presented separately as symbols on their own. Some images show angels holding these objects.

Coins remind us of Judas's betrayal. A crown of thorns is what Roman soldiers put on Jesus' head to mock him for claiming the role of king. A pillar is a symbol of Jesus' scourging, or whipping.

The Holy Lance—a long spear—was used to pierce Jesus' side, from which blood and water flowed. A sponge on the end of a spear reminds us of how, when Jesus said he was thirsty, someone soaked a sponge with sour wine and offered it to him. Soldiers gambled for Jesus' clothes, and so we see a pair of dice.

When Jesus was crucified, he was tied to the cross, and three nails fixed him there—one through each hand and the third through both feet. Quite often, we see the nails and the crown of thorns drawn together.

We are Jesus' friends and want to be like him. This means that we grow in love, and love will sometimes lead us to sacrifice. These symbols of Jesus' death remind us to pray for Jesus' help to keep loving, even when we meet suffering on the way.

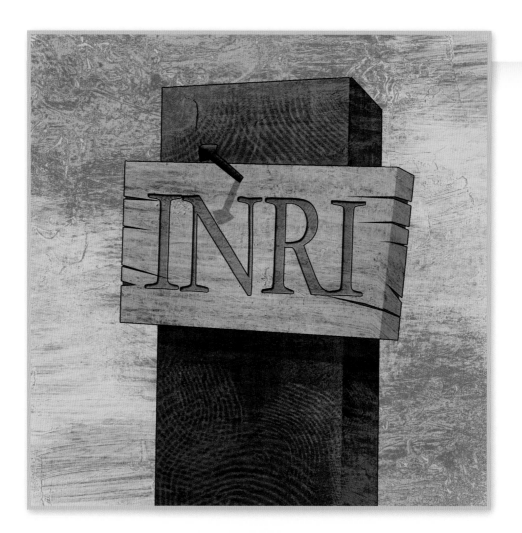

INRI

W hen Jesus hung on the Cross, the Roman authorities nailed a sign above him. That sign read, in Latin, "Jesus the Nazarene, King of the Jews." John and Luke tell us it was written in Hebrew and Greek as well. The abbreviation for the Latin words is *INRI*, which is why we see this written at the top of many crucifixes in churches and homes.

A Closer Look . . .

as Jesus a king? When the Roman governor Pontius Pilate asked him directly, Jesus answered in a puzzling way: "You say so" (Mark 15:2). In John's Gospel, Jesus emphasized that his kingdom is not of this world.

If we have been paying attention to Jesus, his answers here would not surprise us. For we know that Jesus is certainly Lord. He speaks of a unity with the Father and tells us all about the Kingdom of God.

But we also know that he is not a king in the way the world thinks of it. But the world—in the person of the Roman authorities—did decide that Jesus was claiming to be a certain kind of king, and this was a good reason to give in to religious authorities and put him to death.

So they put a sign above his crucified, humiliated body: in Latin it read **Iesus Nazarenus Rex Iudaeorum**: "Jesus the Nazarene, King of the Jews." They intended this as mockery, but friends of Jesus know that he really is king and that the humiliation the Romans intended became a victory instead.

But why an **I** instead of a **J**? The reason is that the letter **J** did not exist until the fourteenth century in English. Latin translated the Hebrew and Greek beginnings of Jesus' name with an **I** that is pronounced, if you have ever heard Latin prayers, like a **Y** in English.

Veil of Veronica

J esus had to carry his cross through Jerusalem on the way to be crucified. It was very crowded in the narrow streets, and some people were weeping to see Jesus suffer. One story tells us about Veronica, a woman who wiped Jesus' sweaty, bloody face with her veil. When she took the cloth away, the image of Jesus' face remained there.

A Closer Look . . .

 e long to see God. But, as the apostle Paul said, "At present we see indistinctly." However, the time will come when we see him face-to-face.

That time has begun in Jesus, who is the face of God. Over the centuries of Christian life, friends of Jesus have drawn closer to God by meditating on the gift of the Incarnation: God become human. They have done this through devotion to the holy face of Jesus. For example, you might have heard of Saint Thérèse of Lisieux. Her full religious name was Saint Thérèse of the Child Jesus and the Holy Face.

When people focus their prayer on the holy face of Jesus, it is the face of the suffering Jesus. The roots of this image go back to traditions that developed in later centuries about a woman who met Jesus, either during his ministry or on his way to Calvary. His face was imprinted on a cloth that she carried, a "true image," or **vera icona** in Latin. Thus, this woman came to be known as "Veronica."

We do not know the historical facts behind any of these traditions, but what we do know is that Jesus was, indeed, the Word made flesh. In his voice, his hands, and his face we find compassion, love, and the true presence of our loving God.

Goldfinch and Pelican

I n hundreds of paintings of Mary and baby Jesus, the child is holding a bird. It is a European goldfinch. This tiny bird, with its bright red head, was a symbol of Jesus' Passion. A legend told that when Jesus wore his crown of thorns, a goldfinch tried to ease his suffering by plucking out thorns and was spattered with Jesus' blood.

A Closer Look . . .

Paintings of the Madonna and Child in medieval times and during the Renaissance often included the tiny European goldfinch. The baby Jesus is depicted holding this small bird with a red head.

This goldfinch was a symbol of Jesus' Passion for two reasons. The first was a natural one: the European goldfinch does eat thistles and thorns. Second, a legend developed in which a goldfinch passing by the suffering Jesus tried to ease his pain by plucking from the crown of thorns; the bird's head is red from Jesus' spattered blood. In pictures of the baby Jesus, the goldfinch reminds us why this child has come to earth. It also points to the virtue of compassion.

The pelican also is associated with Jesus' Passion. People believed that some pelican mothers would feed their starving offspring with blood from their own chest. Even before the time of Jesus, the pelican was a symbol of sacrifice, so it made sense for Christians to associate it with Jesus. In some depictions of the Crucifixion, you will see a pelican's nest resting at the top of the Cross.

Ashes

On Ash Wednesday, which is the beginning of Lent, the priest puts ashes on our foreheads. In ancient Israel, people used ashes to show God they were serious about changing their lives. Ashes remind us that life on earth doesn't last forever. During Lent, we ask God to forgive us and change us so that we can share with him the life that lasts forever.

A Closer Look . . .

shes are what's left after something burns. When we see ashes, we know that there's been change.

When the people of Israel wanted to show God that they had changed—that they had repented of their sins—one of the signs they offered God was ashes. When the king of Nineveh heard the prophet Jonah's warning and repented of sin, he came down from his throne and sat in ashes (Jonah 3:6). God tells his suffering people through the prophet Isaiah that he will replace their ashes with a crown.

Ashes mark the beginning of Lent. They're a sign of our own sorrow for sin, for whatever is standing between us and Easter joy. On Ash Wednesday, we come together to pray, admit our sin, and express sorrow for turning away from God. The ashes we receive on our heads are a sign of that repentance. The ashes are usually burned from the previous year's palms from Palm Sunday. When we receive the ashes, we hear one of two phrases, either "Remember that you are dust and to dust you shall return" or "Repent, and believe in the gospel."

These ashes are a sign that we are willing to burn away all the selfishness and pride and let God's love grow in our hearts in their place. They are a sign, too, of the shortness of life on earth and a reminder to set our hearts on life with God, forever.

Palms

In the ancient world, palm branches were a sign of victory. When Jesus came to Jerusalem, people who had heard about him welcomed him as the Messiah, their Savior who would give them victory. They spread palm branches on the ground in front of him as he rode down the street. Today we begin Holy Week with palms. We sing praise to our Lord Jesus, who has won the victory over sin and death.

A Closer Look . . .

esus had traveled around Palestine preaching, healing, and sharing the good news of God's love. People listened and wondered. They could see that Jesus was clearly a man, but he seemed to be something more. He did things that only God can do—like forgive sins.

One year, as Passover approached, Jesus and his friends traveled to Jerusalem. Crowds of pilgrims and followers came too, and when Jesus entered the city on a donkey, the conviction that Jesus was the Messiah took shape and voice. People sang ancient psalms of praise to God. They cut palm branches and spread them out in front of Jesus as he rode into the city.

Palms were powerful symbols to the people. The large leaves and branches were a sign of victory, and to many ancient cultures they were a sign of peace. The palm branches on that day—the first Palm Sunday—were signs that the people believed God was giving them victory through Jesus.

Jesus did win the greatest victory the world has ever known, the victory it needed more than anything else. When we wave our own blessed palms and sing **Hosanna** to the king on Palm Sunday every year, we're celebrating that most important victory of all: Jesus' victory over sin and death through his Cross.

The Risen Christ

J esus was crucified, but he rose from the dead. In many images of the Resurrection, we see Jesus surrounded by light and wearing white. He still has wounds from the Crucifixion—nail prints in his hands and a wound in his side—but he does not suffer from them anymore. Sometimes in pictures of the Resurrection, Jesus carries a flag with a cross on it, which is a sign of his victory over death.

A Closer Look ...

E arly on Sunday morning, Mary Magdalene walked to Jesus' tomb. She had a difficult, sad job ahead: to finish preparing his body for burial. She wondered how she would move the heavy stone away from the tomb's entrance.

But the stone had already been moved, and the tomb was empty. Soon after, Mary met a man she thought was a gardener. But when he said her name, she recognized that this person was Jesus. He was alive!

Jesus' Resurrection is the center of our Christian faith. We want to have pictures of what happened, but that's not possible because no other human being was there to see it. It's a mystery. When artists depict the Resurrection, they use various symbols to help us understand its meaning.

In these pictures, light comes from Jesus. He still bears the wounds of his Crucifixion, as the Gospels tell us. Usually he wears a white cloth. Jesus might be stepping out of a cave or even out of a sarcophagus, and we might see sleeping guards on the ground nearby. As Jesus steps forward, he might be trampling on bones or a snake, symbols of death and sin.

Some icons show Jesus emerging from Hades, the place of the dead. Images will depict Jesus coming out of Hades, often pulling people up with him. In some pictures, these people are Adam and Eve. There might be a creature down below in chains, which symbolizes death, over which Jesus won the victory. Keys and broken chains indicate the souls that Jesus has set free. Often, Jesus carries a banner with a cross on it, another symbol of the victory he has won for us.

Easter Eggs

E aster is about the new life Jesus shares with us through his Resurrection. We celebrate Easter with symbols that remind us of beautiful new life: baby rabbits, butterflies that have been transformed from caterpillars, and Easter eggs. A chick breaks out of its egg and is born into a new kind of life. This reminds us that Jesus broke out of the tomb to share eternal life with us.

A Closer Look . . .

The goodness of creation reflects the goodness that God wants for us. God wants us to be healthy and at peace; he wants us to be whole and joyful. When Jesus came among us, he healed us, he fed us, and he gave us himself as the way, the truth, and the life. Jesus completed God's plan for creation—God's plan for us.

God didn't create us to sin and suffer death, but through our own choices, we did. When Jesus suffered on the Cross and rose from the dead, he gave us back our real, true selves. The Resurrection was the dawn of a new creation.

When we celebrate Easter and what it really means, we look to God's creation and see its signs of hope, change, and the promise of new life. One sign is one of the simplest, smallest things you can imagine: an egg.

Eggs have symbolized life, health, and hope in many cultures. Christians saw from the beginning that a chick breaking through its shell to new life in the world was a powerful reminder of Jesus breaking free from death and emerging from the tomb. Eggs have been found in ancient Christian tombs. In many cultures, people decorate eggs for Easter, some very elaborately. In some places, especially for Eastern Christians, red is a preferred color for Easter eggs because it reminds us of the blood Jesus shed to give us eternal life.

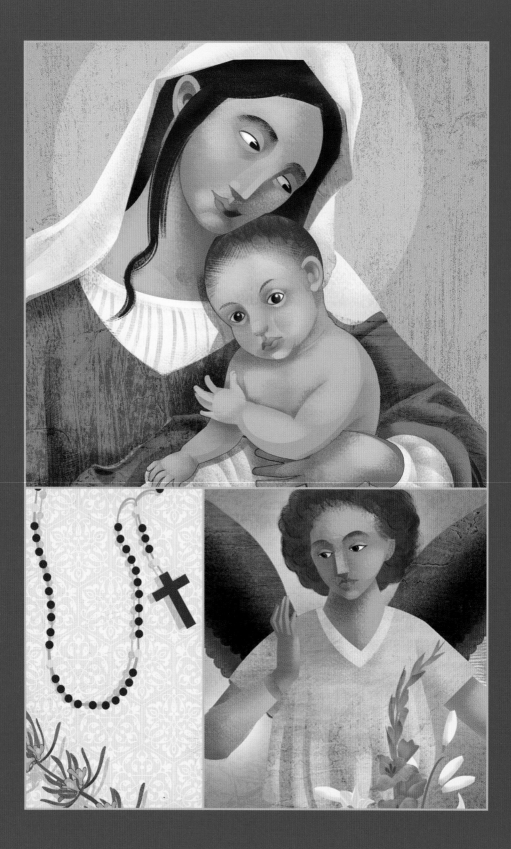

MARY

Mary kept all these things, reflecting on them in her heart.

Luke 2:19

Mary, the mother of Jesus, is a sign all by herself. She's a sign of faith and trust in God. She's a sign of God's generosity and love.

Over the centuries, Christians have drawn close to Mary because when they're close to her, they are close to Jesus, too. Christians have expressed this closeness and their love for Mary in signs and symbols: colors and plants, the human heart, and the most familiar sight of all, one that expresses love, no matter where you live or when: a mother and her child.

Madonna and Child

We call an image of Mary holding the baby Jesus a "Madonna and Child." Artists from around the world like to create pictures, statues, and icons of the Madonna and Child. Jesus, the Son of God, humbled himself and came to earth to live among us. One of the ways we can open ourselves to Jesus' love is by thinking about Jesus as a baby in his mother's arms.

A Closer Look . . .

P ictures of Mary holding the baby Jesus have dominated
Christian art for centuries. We call Mary the **Madonna** from
Italian words that mean "my lady," and so these pictures are
called "Madonna and Child" images.

When artists create these images, they fill them with all kinds
of symbols that are interesting to explore. Do they wear royal-
looking clothes, and are they sitting on a throne? This tells us
that Jesus is Lord and that Mary, his mother, is worthy of honor
too. Or are they dressed more humbly in ordinary surroundings?
This tells us that Jesus was fully human, born of a woman. Are
they looking at each other out of love, or are they looking out
at us, inviting us into their communion? Is Mary pointing to
Jesus? Is she nursing him? What else do we see in the picture?
A goldfinch represents Resurrection; a lamb reminds us of the
Passion. A lily signifies Mary's purity; a violet, her humility.

All these intriguing symbols invite us to enter more deeply the
mystery and grace of God's love come to earth—to every part
of the earth, every culture at every point in time. That's why
people from all regions and cultures have depicted Mary and
Jesus in their own time period, in their own skin: love born
among us—all of us—seen in a mother and child.

Mary in Blue

hen artists create images of Mary, they use colors and symbols to show what Mary means to us. If Mary is dressed in rich, fancy designs, the artist isn't saying that Mary was a rich woman in real life. They want to show people of their time that Mary is important. When we see Mary dressed in a blue mantle, or cloak, as she often is, that's a symbol too. It's a symbol of the heavens and Mary's prayers for us, prayers offered so close to the heart of God.

A Closer Look . . .

 ver the centuries, certain colors came to have symbolism in general and related to the Blessed Virgin Mary specifically.

We associate the color blue with Mary. Many images that we see in our churches present Mary wearing a blue mantle, or cloak. Blue is a symbol of the heavens. Mary helps us come closer to God, so it makes sense that she'd wear blue. In the late Middle Ages and the Renaissance, a certain kind of blue was the most expensive and rare pigment an artist could buy. Painting Mary's mantle with this substance was a sign of how special she was.

But Mary wears other colors, too. She might wear white as a symbol of purity or black in scenes of the Crucifixion. She might wear red, symbolizing her human nature, or, in some cultures, indicating her nobility in God's kingdom. It's important to remember that when artists paint Mary wearing certain designs or colors, they're not trying to show us what a poor woman in first-century Galilee wore. They're trying to tell us, through color and design, who she is: that she's pure of heart, full of grace, close to God, and nobler than any earthly queen.

Mary and the Serpent

Every Catholic church has at least one statue of the Blessed Virgin Mary. When we look at the statues of Mary, we see her reaching out to us. She's standing on a small globe or perhaps on a crescent moon. Sometimes she stands on a snake. That's the serpent in the Garden of Eden who tempted Eve to disobey God. When we see Mary stepping on it, we remember that through Mary's yes to God, Jesus came into the world and conquered sin.

A Closer Look . . .

The Book of Genesis tells the story of hope, sadness—and then new hope. We read of God's love in creating the universe and how what he created is good. But then the people God created reject all that goodness and choose sin instead. That's not the end of the story, though. In Genesis chapter 3, there's a glimmer of hope.

As God tells Adam, Eve, and the serpent the consequences of their actions, he tells the serpent who had tempted Eve that there would be enmity between him and the woman. Someday the serpent would strike at her heel, but the woman and her offspring would strike at the serpent's head.

This is the very first announcement of the coming of Jesus. It's even called the "first Gospel" by early church fathers. Evil would not win the final victory. This is why many statues and other images of Mary show her stepping on a serpent. She is like a new Eve, driving darkness and sin away rather than inviting it into her life. Sometimes the globe of the earth might be under her feet. This reminds us that every person in every part of the world shares this hope. Through Mary's offspring, Jesus, all people can receive the grace to resist temptation that's held out to us and live in hope and trust in God instead.

Roses and Rosemary

C hristians have long thought of Mary as the loveliest of God's human creations. Flowers, then, are a way for Christians to express and imagine who Mary is. People have planted whole gardens dedicated to flowers that remind them of Mary. Roses are important in images of Mary. Red roses symbolize her sorrows, white her purity, and gold or yellow roses, her glory in heaven. Mary is sometimes called a "rose without thorns" because she was born free of Original Sin.

A Closer Look . . .

hrough history, Christians have associated Mary with plants that are beautiful and life giving. Most of these plants are flowers, and the most well-known is the rose.

To the Romans, roses symbolized beauty and triumphant love, so it was not a big step for Christians to connect roses with Mary. You will often see Mary crowned with roses or her heart circled with roses. And, of course, our great devotion to Mary—the Rosary—gets its name from roses.

Red roses remind us of Mary's suffering, yellow or gold her glory in heaven, and white, her purity.

The rosemary plant is not related to roses, but a legend connects it to Mary. Rosemary is an herb that grows into large bushes. The story says that when the Holy Family fled to Egypt, Mary spread her cloak to dry on the rosemary bush, and the plant then absorbed the sweet scent of her goodness.

There are so many plants named after Mary that you could fill a garden with them. In fact, for hundreds of years, people have done just that. "Mary Gardens" contain flowers and herbs that remind people of some quality of the Blessed Virgin.

Lily and Gladiolus

I n May, the earth comes to life again with new green leaves and bright flowers. This lovely new life reminds us of Mary, so May is her month too. One of the many flowers that remind us of Mary is the lily. A lily is a symbol of purity. The shape of the gladiolus leaf is like a sword, which represents the sorrow Mary felt when her son suffered and died.

A Closer Look . . .

ary Gardens are filled with plants associated with her, and the month of flowering—May—is Mary's month.

The lily is a large white flower you will often see in images of Mary, especially in pictures of the Annunciation, the moment in which the angel Gabriel told Mary she'd be the mother of the Messiah. In these images, the angel holds a lily, or there is a lily in a vase nearby. One kind of lily, called the Madonna lily, has a white body that symbolizes Mary's purity and gold inner parts that symbolize her soul, full of grace. The Assumption lily is named thus because it blooms only around the time of the Feast of the Assumption, August 15.

The blossoms of the gladiolus are big and bright, arrayed in rows around a long stem. The stem looks like a sword, so when people look at the gladiolus, it reminds them of Mary's sorrows piercing her beautiful heart, as Simeon prophesied. The lady's slipper symbolizes Mary going on foot to visit Elizabeth. The marigold is named after Mary, the woman clothed with the gold of the sun.

Immaculate Heart of Mary

Luke's Gospel tells us that after Jesus' birth, Mary kept all that she had seen and heard in her heart. Images of Mary's Immaculate Heart have a flame because it burns with love. Her heart is surrounded by a crown of roses, which reminds us of beauty and suffering. A sword piercing Mary's heart is a symbol of the sorrow she will suffer when Jesus is crucified.

A Closer Look . . .

T he heart is the mysterious place that is the center of our feelings and understanding. Keeping Mary's heart as a part of our prayer helps us draw closer to her and, because she is the mother of Jesus, to her Son. Luke tells us of the importance of Mary's heart. He mentions how she remembered and contemplated in her heart what she had experienced of Jesus as a baby and a child (Luke 2:19, 51).

We call Mary's heart the Immaculate Heart because she was conceived without Original Sin and remained full of grace, belonging to God her whole life.

Love is intense and powerful, which is why it is represented by a flame coming from Mary's heart. When Mary and Joseph presented the baby Jesus at the Temple, the prophet Simeon told her that a sword would pierce her heart at the way the world would react to Jesus. So images of Mary's heart often have at least one sword and sometimes seven because Christians have found it fruitful to contemplate Mary's seven sorrows—or **dolors:**

1. The prophecy of Simeon
2. The flight into Egypt
3. The loss of the Child Jesus in the Temple
4. The meeting of Jesus and Mary on the Way of the Cross
5. The Crucifixion
6. The taking down of the Body of Jesus from the Cross
7. The burial of Jesus

The Immaculate Heart is surrounded by a ring of roses or thorns. That is a symbol of Mary's suffering as she watched her Son endure pain for us.

Our Lady of Guadalupe

L ong ago, near what is now Mexico City, a poor man had a vision. His name was Juan Diego, and in his vision he saw the Blessed Virgin Mary. When the religious authorities doubted Juan Diego's story, he showed them his coat. On it was a miraculous image of the Blessed Virgin. She stands on the crescent moon, and the rays of the sun surround her. She looks like one of the native people, with darker skin and hair. This was a sign to Juan Diego's people that the Christian faith was meant for them, too.

A Closer Look . . .

Several hundred years ago, Christianity had just been brought to the Americas. It was certainly good news to bring Jesus to those who didn't know him, but the way it had been brought could make it hard to understand that Christianity really was good news. After all, the people bringing this faith were conquerors, and the indigenous peoples were treated harshly as the foreign government forces took control of the land.

Then, in 1531, truly good news came to the indigenous people in this complicated situation. Not far from what is now Mexico City, on a hill called Tepayac, a native of that land, a man named Juan Diego, had a vision of the Blessed Virgin Mary. She told him to tell the local bishop to build a shrine on that spot. The bishop did not believe Juan Diego, and so as a sign, when Juan Diego opened his coat, roses spilled out. On his coat, or **tilma**, was imprinted the image of the Blessed Virgin.

The shrine was constructed, and it's there you can see the **tilma** and its image today. Mary is surrounded by symbols of the heavens: she stands on the crescent moon with the sun's rays around her, and her turquoise garment shines with stars. Mary looks down humbly, and most important, her complexion is dark—she looks like Juan Diego's people. This is a sign that the Good News she bears—her son, Jesus—is for everyone, all over the world.

Our Lady of Perpetual Help

O*ur Lady of Perpetual Help* is the name of an ancient icon in a small church in Rome. In the picture, Jesus has just come to Mary for comfort, in such a hurry that his sandal has fallen off. Above them are angels carrying symbols of the death Jesus will suffer. Mary is looking at us, and in her eyes we see that she understands our suffering.

A Closer Look . . .

 Mary, mother of Jesus and his first disciple, shows us the way to God's mercy. To people all over the world, she is "Our Lady" and we trust that she is praying for us in all our different situations. We might know her as Our Lady of Lourdes, Our Lady of Fatima, Our Lady, Star of the Sea. We might think of her for what she shows us through Jesus: Our Lady of Mercy, Our Lady of Grace, Our Lady of Victory.

One of Mary's titles—Our Lady of Perpetual Help—is related to an icon of Mary and Jesus that emerged in the Middle Ages and was displayed in a church in Rome. For three centuries it was venerated there; many people received help and encouragement when they drew near to Mary and Jesus as they prayed before this image. When the church was destroyed in an invasion, the icon was lost for many years but was then discovered, restored, and placed in a new church in the 1860s. People continue to find great comfort and even miracles in this image and its symbolism. Copies of the icon are used in prayer and devotions all over the world.

In this picture, Mary and Jesus are seated against a background of gold, the color of heavenly glory. Jesus is sitting rather anxiously in his mother's arms. One of his sandals has fallen off, and he is clutching her hand. He is looking up at the angels Michael and Gabriel, who are carrying the instruments of his coming Passion: nails, a cross, a lance, and a sponge. Mary is looking at us. She receives Jesus, and she presents him to us. She is comforting Jesus, but she wants to comfort us, too.

SAINTS

*"Good teacher, what must I do
to inherit eternal life?"*

Mark 10:17

 saint is a person who was a friend of God on earth and who now dwells with God in heaven. There are thousands of saints from all times and places. Saints are young and old, women and men, rich and poor, busy and quiet.

We like to have pictures of our friends with us. When we keep images of saints in our homes and churches, we're remembering how close they are to us. They care for us and want to help us still, and they do so by their example and their prayers. Because we don't know what most of the saints looked like, when artists draw, paint, or sculpt a saint's image, they often include a symbol specific to that saint's life.

John the Baptist

P eople came from all over the country to hear John the Baptist preach. He baptized those who decided to turn from their sins. He told of another person, greater than him, who would soon come to them. When Jesus came to John for baptism, John knew that this was the Lamb of God who would take away the sin of the world. In pictures, John wears rough clothing made of camel's hair. He sometimes holds a staff that has a cross on it, and there is sometimes a lamb nearby.

A Closer Look . . .

 We call John the Baptist the "forerunner" because he was the prophetic voice who prepared the way for Jesus. John, who was Jesus' cousin, went into the wilderness and lived a simple, hard life focused on God's will. He preached repentance, and people came to him for baptism in the Jordan River. Jesus came, too, to have John baptize him at the beginning of his public ministry.

John is easy to recognize in art. Usually he's dressed in the camel's-hair tunic and leather belt the Gospels describe him as wearing. Because John called Jesus "the Lamb of God, who takes away the sin of the world," a lamb might be present. John usually carries a staff, and that staff is in the shape of a cross. Sometimes the staff has a banner attached to it.

John appears in some portraits of the baby Jesus and his mother. You know the other child is John because, even in these pictures, the little child is dressed in camel's hair and holds a staff or a lamb! The artist does not mean that the baby John was present at Jesus' birth. The image of the two babies reminds us that John's holy purpose was to share the Good News of Jesus, the Lamb of God.

Joseph

T he Gospels tell us that Joseph was Mary's husband and Jesus' earthly father. He was a carpenter who lived in Nazareth. He took Mary to Bethlehem, where Jesus was born. Then, when the family was in danger, Joseph followed God's instructions and took them to live in Egypt for a few years. We think Joseph died before Jesus began traveling and teaching. In pictures of Joseph, he sometimes holds carpenter tools.

A Closer Look . . .

T he Gospel of Matthew tells us that Joseph was already betrothed to Mary when he found out she was having a baby. After an angel came to him in a dream and told him that the child was conceived by the Holy Spirit, Joseph took Mary as his wife and cared for her and the child Jesus. We don't know much more about Joseph than that. Because he's not mentioned later, we think he died before Jesus began his public ministry.

We don't know how old Joseph was when Jesus was born. Different stories and traditions have influenced the way artists depict him. Some traditions say that Joseph was a widower, and so he is portrayed as old, even elderly. In other settings, Joseph is closer to Mary's age, but still a little older, an adult who is strong and capable of caring for his family.

The Gospels refer to Jesus as "the carpenter's son," so Joseph is portrayed holding the tools of the carpenter's trade, often the L-shaped measuring tool called a carpenter's square. In some pictures, Joseph holds a staff flowering with lilies, which is a sign that God has chosen him. In the Book of Numbers, God gave this same sign when he chose Aaron to help Moses: he made a staff sprout flower blossoms. The lilies from Joseph's staff also symbolize that Joseph and Mary were pure in their dedication to God's will.

Peter and Paul

P eter was a fisherman Jesus called to follow him. His name
was Simon, but Jesus gave him a new name that means
"rock." Jesus told Peter that he was giving him the keys to the
kingdom, which means Peter was the leader of the Apostles.
That's why many pictures of Peter show him holding keys.
Paul carries a sword as a symbol of his martyrdom and a book
representing the letters he wrote to churches.

A Closer Look . . .

S imon was a fisherman on the Sea of Galilee. One day, Jesus approached Simon and his brother Andrew and told him he would make him a fisher of people. Simon, Andrew, and their friends James and John, also brothers and fishermen, left everything and followed Jesus. They were the first of the Twelve Apostles.

There was more in store for Simon. Jesus called him to be a leader of the Apostles, and as we understand now, the leader of the whole Church: the first pope. In Scripture stories, when God calls a person to something new, God might change that person's name. This was so with Simon, whom Jesus renamed **Peter** (**Petros** in Greek), a name that means "rock." Jesus also said he was giving Peter the "keys to the kingdom" of God—authority to act in his name.

That is why we recognize Peter in art by the keys he holds. Sometimes you will see a rooster nearby, a symbol of that sad night when Peter denied Jesus three times before the rooster crowed, just as Jesus had predicted.

After Paul's dramatic conversion to faith in Jesus, he spent his life traveling from country to country and church to church, teaching and encouraging the believers.

Peter and Paul are often portrayed together, maybe holding a small church building between them as a sign that they helped build up the Church. Paul will have a sword to symbolize that he was martyred by beheading. He carries a book as a reminder that he wrote many letters to Christians of various churches; some of these letters we know as Epistles in the New Testament.

Mary Magdalene

Mary Magdalene was a disciple of Jesus. He had freed her from evil spirits, and she followed him. She watched Jesus die on the Cross, and she was the first of Jesus' friends to see him after the Resurrection, when she went to his tomb to finish preparing his body with oils and spices. In art, Mary Magdalene often wears red. There is nearly always a jar of oil close by or in her hand.

A Closer Look . . .

n the first day of the week, Mary Magdalene approached Jesus' tomb. She was there to finish the sad job of preparing his body for burial with spices, oils, and clean cloths. Mary had been with Jesus since he freed her from seven evil spirits. She was present at the Crucifixion and saw Jesus die. On this morning, Mary was surprised, for there on the path, she met the risen Lord!

When we see Mary Magdalene in art, it is usually in one of these Gospel scenes. We recognize her because of the red robe or gown she wears and because of the jar she carries. This is the oil Mary used to anoint Jesus for burial. Ancient Christian tradition also associated Mary Magdalene with other women who anointed Jesus' feet in love and repentance (Luke 7, John 12). Because Mary Magdalene often symbolizes repentance, artists will show her thinking about her past sins. In these scenes, you will find not only a jar but also a skull, which symbolizes the shortness of earthly life.

In some images, Mary Magdalene holds a red egg. The egg was a symbol of the Resurrection. And in one early legend, Mary traveled to Rome after Jesus' Ascension and had dinner with Tiberius Caesar. When she told him of Jesus' Resurrection, he scoffed and said that a person could no more rise from the dead than the egg she held in her hand could turn red. The egg immediately turned red.

The Twelve Apostles

F or the Jewish people, the number 12 was a sign of something being complete, or perfect. Jacob had twelve sons, who became the fathers of the twelve tribes of Israel. Jesus called twelve apostles to take his Good News out to the world. In these scenes, sometimes all the Apostles look very similar, but you can usually recognize at least two: Peter, with a short curly beard—or a gray-haired, older man—and John, who looks the youngest and has no beard or mustache.

A Closer Look . . .

 esus had many followers during his earthly ministry, but at the center were The Twelve. These were the Apostles, called by Jesus to leave behind everything in their ordinary lives to follow him. There were twelve tribes at the core of God's people under the old covenant. In the same way, there are twelve apostles— the first bishops—at the core of the new covenant.

In art we see the Twelve Apostles represented in scenes of Jesus' ministry of preaching and healing, but most often they are all together as a group at the Last Supper or—without Judas and before Matthias had been elected to replace him—at Pentecost. We also see them in scenes of heaven, surrounding Jesus closely, sometimes seated on thrones.

There are many traditions about the ministries of the Apostles after Jesus' Ascension, and we see these traditions about the Apostles' evangelizing journeys represented in art. In some images we can recognize an Apostle because he is holding something related to the way he was martyred: Saint Andrew with a cross in the shape of an X, for example, and Saint Bartholomew holding his own skin because tradition tells us that in Armenia where he ministered, he was executed by being skinned alive.

The Four Evangelists

Jesus brings Good News to you and me and the whole world. During his life, people listened carefully to this Good News and passed it on to others. Then they wrote it down so that people in the future could know Jesus, too. The four Gospels were written by Matthew, Mark, Luke, and John. You might see their symbols in a church or on the cover of a Bible. Matthew's symbol is a man; Mark's is a lion; Luke's is an ox; and John's is an eagle. They all have wings.

A Closer Look . . .

The Book of Revelation is the last book in the Bible. In it, we read a long, complicated but rich vision of the end of time and life in heaven. In one part of that vision, we see a throne—the throne of the Lord—and surrounding the throne are many kinds of beings, all singing praise to God.

Close to the throne are four living creatures, each with six wings and many eyes. Each of the four resemble something different: a human being, a lion, an ox, and an eagle.

Early Christian writers found much to think and pray about in the Book of Revelation. The symbols in this book helped them deepen their understanding of the mystery of God and his will for creation. It seemed that these four living, winged creatures were like the four writers of the Gospels, whom we call the four Evangelists.

Matthew's Gospel reminded them of the humanlike creature because he begins his Gospel with the human family background of Jesus.

Mark is associated with the lion, a symbol of courage and of resurrection. Luke has been represented by the ox, partly because the ox was a symbol of sacrifices offered to the Lord, and Luke's Gospel begins with Zechariah, John the Baptist's father, ministering in the Temple.

John's Gospel begins not with the earth but with the heavens, as he describes Jesus' divine nature as the Word of God. So the eagle, soaring high in the sky, represents John.

Martyrs

Christian martyrs are people who have been killed because of their faith. By being willing to die, they show us that God is real and powerful and that they trust him. Many saints are martyrs, and pictures of them show certain symbols. The martyr holds a palm branch, because in the ancient world, the palm was a symbol of victory. An angel near the martyr might hold a palm branch.

A Closer Look . . .

e've heard that "actions speak louder than words." No matter what you say you believe, you demonstrate your true beliefs and priorities through what you do.

Some people show by their actions that God is more important to them than anything else. They are willing to give up anything for God, even life itself. People who have been executed because of their faith are called martyrs. The word **martyr** means "witness"; through his or her sacrifice, a martyr gives witness to the truth of the faith.

Not all saints are martyrs, but many are, and we can recognize them in art because of certain symbols. The palm was a symbol of victory in the ancient world. Martyrs, although they seem defeated, are victorious over the temptation to give in to the world's demands. Through Christ, they are victorious over death. In many martyr images, the martyr or an angel close by holds a palm branch. Angels might carry to the martyr a crown of victory, sometimes made of roses.

A martyr is also depicted with the symbol of his or her death. Saint Stephen would have stones; Saint Lucy carries her eyes on a dish; and Saint Lawrence holds a gridiron upon which the Roman authorities tortured him. No matter how they died, they gave their lives for their faith and because they loved God.

Francis of Assisi

F rancis of Assisi was born into a wealthy family, but God called him to something greater. Francis gave his life completely to God. He followed Jesus' example and chose a life of poverty and humility. Images of Saint Francis show him wearing the brown Franciscan robe tied with a rope belt. There will be a cross or crucifix nearby, and on Francis's hands and feet you might see marks like those of Jesus on the Cross.

A Closer Look . . .

Saint Francis of Assisi is one of Christianity's most popular saints. In his example we see the joy that comes from giving our lives completely to God and trusting in him.

In art we see various scenes of Francis's life: his steps away from his earthly family, his embrace of lepers, his preaching, his interaction with animals, his creation of the first Nativity scene in Greccio, and his death, humbly laid on God's earth, as he had requested.

We can recognize Saint Francis in these and other pieces of art because he is slightly built and wears the brown Franciscan robe with a rope belt. In many images, you will see a wolf nearby, a reminder of how Francis was able to tame a wolf that was terrorizing the village called Gubbio. A skull, a symbol of the shortness of earthly life, might also be in the picture. There will also be a cross or crucifix, the most powerful sign of Jesus' love and humility that Francis sought to imitate.

Francis's communion with the crucified Christ was so strong that, late in his short life, Francis began to bear on his body the signs of this love: the wounds of Jesus' Crucifixion, called the **stigmata**.

Jerome

Saint Jerome was a scholar and a hermit who lived in the Holy Land to pray, study, and translate the Bible from Hebrew and Greek into Latin. In art, Jerome is usually a thin, older man, and he wears very few clothes. Or, he might wear the red robe and hat of a cardinal. Often in these pictures, there's a lion near Saint Jerome. One legend tells us that he helped a lion that was wounded. To repay Jerome's kindness, the lion stayed by his side in the monastery.

A Closer Look . . .

The books of the Bible were inspired by the Holy Spirit but were written in the human languages of Hebrew and Greek. As the People of God spread into different cultures, the Bible had to be translated. The most important early translator of the Bible was Saint Jerome, who lived during the fourth century. He was a scholar and monk who settled in the Holy Land, outside of Bethlehem, and took as his life's task the translation of the books of the Bible into Latin. We call this translation the Vulgate, and for centuries it was the most important Bible translation for Catholics.

Most pictures of Saint Jerome show him as a thin older man with a long white beard, and usually he doesn't have many clothes on; that's a sign that he's a hermit. He's writing and studying, and you will probably see a skull and an hourglass nearby. It is common to see a skull in a picture of a saint. It's a reminder that the saint is focused on God, who is eternal, and not on the things of this world, which pass away.

And almost every time you see Saint Jerome in a picture, you'll see a lion, too, sitting close to him. The story is told that Jerome took the thorn out of a paw of a lion who had wandered into his monastery, and in gratitude, the lion stayed with Jerome for the rest of his days.

Anthony of Padua

S aint Anthony of Padua was a Franciscan friar and a great preacher. In art, especially statues, we see him in the brown Franciscan habit. He had a vision of the child Jesus, so some images show him carrying the Christ Child, sometimes on top of a book, which symbolizes Anthony's learning. He often carries a lily, which symbolizes purity. We pray to Saint Anthony to help us find lost objects.

A Closer Look . . .

Saint Anthony of Padua was born in Lisbon, Portugal, and as a young man joined the Augustinian religious order. He was inspired, though, by the simple lifestyle of some nearby Franciscans, and when he heard about the martyrdom of five Franciscans who had gone to Morocco to evangelize, he knew that his call was with Saint Francis's brotherhood of humility and simplicity.

Anthony ended up in Italy, where Saint Francis heard about his gifts for scholarship and preaching and recommended Anthony to teach theology to other Franciscan brothers. Anthony became known for his understanding of Scripture, for his powerful preaching, and for various miracles associated with him. He died of an illness at age thirty-six.

Anthony is a very popular saint and the patron of lost objects. We often pray for Saint Anthony to help us find misplaced things because, a story tells us, once Anthony couldn't find one of his important books. Another friar, who was running away, had stolen it. But after Anthony appeared to him in a dream, the friar came back—and returned Anthony's book to him.

Images show him dressed in the brown Franciscan robe. Because Anthony had a vision of the infant Jesus, he is often depicted carrying the Christ Child. And sometimes the Christ Child—the Word made flesh—sits on top of an open Bible. This reminds us of Anthony's dedication to sharing the Good News.

Saint Anthony often appears holding a lily, a symbol of purity. One story tells of Saint Anthony receiving a lily from Saint Joseph, who also carried Jesus in his arms.

Thérèse of Lisieux

S aint Thérèse of Lisieux, a Carmelite nun, died when she was only twenty-four years old. A few years later, she was made a saint, and her spiritual writings were read around the world. People love Saint Thérèse because of her humility and her good cheer even during suffering. Images show her in her brown habit. She carries a crucifix because of her love for Jesus, and roses because she is known as "the Little Flower."

A Closer Look . . .

I n the late nineteenth century in northern France, the Martin family had five daughters. All of them eventually joined religious orders, four of them at the nearby Carmelite convent. One of these four took the name Sister Thérèse of the Child Jesus and the Holy Face. She became a saint: Saint Thérèse of Lisieux.

Thérèse was a loving, passionate, and honest young woman. She developed a path of spirituality she called "the Little Way." Sometimes we think that the only important actions in life are those that a lot of people notice. Saint Thérèse reminds us that every moment of every day gives us a chance to love, even in small ways. That is where we follow Jesus—in those small moments on that Little Way.

Thérèse compared herself to a tiny flower, blooming wherever God had planted her, which is why we call her "the Little Flower." She loved roses, and she said that after she died, she would send a "shower of roses" from heaven in the form of her prayers for those of us still on earth. When we see statues and other images of Saint Thérèse, we see, first of all, her brown Carmelite habit, the symbol of a life totally dedicated to Jesus. She carries a crucifix, a symbol of Jesus' suffering. Thérèse believed that her own suffering from tuberculosis brought her closer to Jesus. And, of course, she carries roses.

Halos

I n art, we often see light coming from a person who is close to God. Sometimes the rays surround the person's whole body, as with the image of Our Lady of Guadalupe. But in other images, the light surrounds a person's head. These are called halos. When artists portrayed God the Father, they sometimes gave him a triangle-shaped halo as a sign of the Trinity. Saints' heads were surrounded with circular halos or simple rays.

A Closer Look . . .

 hen you meet a person who is filled with goodness and love, you can just sense it. But you can't draw or sculpt that kind of inner goodness, so artists use signs and symbols to introduce us to people who are especially close to God.

God is the light who shows us the truth about who we are and why we are here, so when artists want to communicate someone's closeness to God, they'll bring light into the picture in specific ways. Sometimes a figure might be surrounded by light, but most of the time, the light surrounds the person's head. We call this a halo, or **nimbus**, which means "cloud."

The shape of a halo tells us something about who we are seeing. Often, halos around Jesus' head have rays of light shaped like a cross. God the Father is not often depicted in art, but when he is, we might see a triangle-shaped halo around his head, which is a symbol of the Trinity.

Saints get halos, too, and these are usually in a circular form, which is a reminder of how close the person is to the eternal God, who has no beginning or end. The style of that circle will depend on the era in which the art was made and on how natural a scene the artist is trying to portray. In art after the Middle Ages, often a saint's halo was soft rays of light.

Relics

S aints are friends of Jesus who share his love through their actions and words, helping others feel closer to Jesus. We believe in the Communion of Saints, which means that a saint can help us even after his or her earthly life has ended. We treasure relics of saints who have died: parts of their bodies, their clothes, and other things that have touched them. Every altar contains relics of a saint. It's a sign that we're all connected, here on earth and in heaven, too.

A Closer Look . . .

 e live on this earth in our bodies; we know each other through our bodies; and we change the world with our bodies. That's what saints do: they use the gift of their bodies to share the love of Jesus.

Death can't stop this love. Even though we're on earth and they're in heaven, we believe in the Communion of Saints. We can still talk to them, and they can still share the love of Jesus with us, through their prayers and even through what's left of their bodies here on earth. We call those **relics**.

There are three kinds of relics. First-class relics are parts of a saint's body. Second-class relics are objects they owned or touched, such as their clothes. Third-class relics are objects— usually a piece of cloth—that's been touched to one of the first two types.

Every altar in a Catholic church must have relics of a saint embedded into the altar stone. Many churches and chapels have relics on display in containers called **reliquaries**. Relics aren't magic. When we pray in the presence of a relic, we are in close communion with a friend of Jesus who is still present and who is helping us here on earth. As Saint Paul says, because of Jesus' victory, death has no more power over us.

OLD TESTAMENT: STORY OF GOD'S PEOPLE

They shall be my people,
and I will be their God.

Jeremiah 32:38

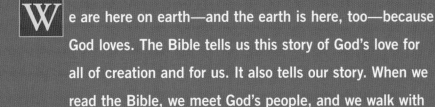e are here on earth—and the earth is here, too—because God loves. The Bible tells us this story of God's love for all of creation and for us. It also tells our story. When we read the Bible, we meet God's people, and we walk with them on their journey.

These stories are filled with signs and symbols: trees, an ark, a dove, plants, mountains, and more. We know the stories. We know the symbols, too—so when we catch a glimpse in a picture in a book or in church, we're glad, because we can remember the story of God's love, a story that we're part of now too.

Tree of Knowledge of Good and Evil

G od created a world full of beauty, and he made human beings in God's image. We can love, create, think, and choose. He put us into the garden of his creation, and he gave us a choice: to follow him and find peace or to follow our own will and wander away from him. When we see the Tree of Knowledge of Good and Evil from the Garden of Eden, we remember who God created us to be, and how saying yes to God brings happiness.

A Closer Look . . .

 mong all his creatures, God gave our first parents something unique: the gift of free will. This, along with the ability to love, create, and reason, are what being created in God's image is all about.

But the happiness of Paradise did not last long. Eve was tempted by the serpent to eat from the one forbidden tree in the garden: the Tree of Knowledge of Good and Evil. To eat from this tree would be an act of disobedience. It would be a way of saying that we know better than God—that we, not God, have the power and the right to decide what's right and wrong.

Our first parents gave in to the temptation, rejected the gift of living in harmony with God and each other, and so had to leave the garden. That's what we see in this tree: our pride and the temptation to say no to our loving Creator. Genesis doesn't say that the fruit on the tree was an apple, although it is usually symbolized that way today. Sometimes when we see the serpent on the tree, he is drawn with legs, for Genesis tells us that one of the serpent's punishments afterward was to crawl on his belly.

This tree stands as a reminder of the sadness of saying no to God. But Christians have always remembered another tree, too: the tree of the Cross, the sign of "yes" through the loving sacrifice of Jesus.

Ark and Dove and Rainbow

S in had destroyed the beauty of God's creation. God decided
to destroy the world with a great Flood and allow people to
start over. God told Noah to build an ark to save his family
and the animals of the world. After the Flood, when the waters
went down, a dove brought to Noah an olive branch, a sign
that life was returning. God made a covenant with Noah, and
a rainbow is a sign that God will never destroy the earth with
floodwaters again.

A Closer Look . . .

 od made the world beautiful and good and created human beings to take care of it and each other. But human beings turned away from God and started hurting one another. The Book of Genesis tells us that sin spread and infected the whole world, so God decided it was time to start over.

Noah's family had remained friends with God. God instructed Noah to build an ark for them and pairs of every animal on earth. The ark saved them from the Flood. After forty days and nights of rain and then months of resting on the floodwaters, Noah sent out birds to find signs of life. Finally, a dove returned with an olive branch. When life on earth was restored, Noah gave thanks to God. God made a covenant with him—a promise that God would never again send a flood to destroy the earth. All covenants are marked with signs, and the sign of this covenant was a rainbow (Genesis 9:8–17).

When we see an image of Noah's ark, it is a sign of salvation. God saves us from the dangers of sin and death. His grace is like an ark for us, safe and warm. It's even a symbol of Baptism, the moment when we come out of the waters, clean and ready for a new life. We see a dove, an olive branch, and a rainbow, and we are reminded that even in the midst of danger, God offers signs of hope.

Burning Bush

God's people were suffering. The Pharaoh of Egypt had turned them into slaves and treated them harshly. Who would help them? God had a plan. He chose Moses to lead his people out of slavery. As a sign of who he was, God appeared to Moses in the form of a bush that was on fire—but the fire didn't destroy it! On that day, from the burning bush, God told Moses his name: I am who I am.

A Closer Look . . .

 od had called and formed his people, first through Abraham. Abraham and his descendants had settled in the Promised Land. When famine struck, God's people traveled to Egypt, where they found food saved by God's providence through Joseph, the son of Jacob.

But now, generations later, Pharaoh had turned against them. Threatened by their large population, he had enslaved the people of Israel. They yearned to be free and return to the Promised Land. God heard their cries and chose a man to lead them to freedom: Moses.

God first appeared to Moses while he was out tending sheep. Moses saw a bush on fire, but strangely, it was not being burnt up by the flames. He approached, and from the burning bush, he heard God calling him to help his people.

As a sign, so the people would trust Moses and know it was God who had called him, God revealed his name from the bush: **I am who I am**. This means that God has not been created—God **is** existence.

When we see the symbol of the burning bush, we remember God's love, always ready to save. We remember that he called Moses and gave him the strength and grace to help others. And we remember how great God is, and we thank him for the gift of life—all that was, all that is, and all that is to come.

Stone Tablets

God made his first covenant with the people through Abraham. Centuries later, through Moses's leadership, God freed the people from slavery in Egypt. Out in the wilderness, on a mountain called Sinai, God came to Moses and gave him the Ten Commandments written on tablets of stone. These laws would guide God's people to a happy and peaceful life.

A Closer Look . . .

T he world is a messy, confusing place, with many voices telling us where to find happiness. Centuries ago, on a mountain in the wilderness in the Middle East, God showed his people the way to true and lasting happiness.

Moses had led the people out of slavery in Egypt. For years they journeyed toward the Promised Land. On the way, they learned, suffered, and grew stronger. On that journey back to the land God had given them, they arrived at a great mountain: Mount Sinai. There, on behalf of the people, Moses had a dramatic encounter with the Lord.

The Lord called Moses up to the mountain amidst thunder and lightning and other signs of his power. There he gave Moses the core of the Law—the Ten Commandments—etched on tablets of stone.

The laws were a gift from God that guided the people back to the life he had intended for them all along: a life centered on loving God and other people. This life brings peace and happiness.

When we see the symbol of these tablets, we remember this gift from God. We are reminded that in the confusion of the world, God hasn't been silent. He gives us the gift of happiness and peace, and it's as solid as stone.

The Number 40

I n the Bible, the number 40 often represents a time of testing or trial. For forty days and nights it rained on Noah, his family, and the ark. Moses and the Israelites were in the desert for forty years. After Jesus was baptized, he spent forty days and nights in the desert praying—and he was tempted by the Devil. Forty can symbolize a challenge, but it also reminds us that God is with us through the challenge.

A Closer Look . . .

hen Christians hear the number 3, they think of God—the Holy Trinity. The number 7 communicates fullness and completion, as with God's creation of the world in seven days.

We see the number 40 quite often in the history of God's people. The rains of the flood lasted for forty days and forty nights. After God freed them from slavery in Egypt, the people of Israel wandered in the wilderness for forty years before they finally reached the Promised Land that God had given their ancestors. During that time in the wilderness, Moses went up Mount Sinai where he encountered God. These times of encounter lasted forty days.

In all these situations, **forty** meant trial and testing. The forty days or weeks were times in which people were challenged to focus more deeply on God. During the forty days or forty years of testing, they grew in strength and came to a better understanding of themselves and God's purpose for them.

We live the meaning of **forty** today. During Lent, we follow Jesus into the desert, where he stayed for forty days. Like him, we fast and pray. We accept suffering and grow stronger in it. We deepen our love for God, and we ready ourselves to serve him with joy.

Mountains

H igh on a mountain, Moses met God in thunder and lightning. Years later, on another mountain, the prophet Elijah met God in a quiet whisper. God's ways are higher than our ways. That's why mountains are signs of close meetings with God. When the prophets describe what life will be like with God at the end of time, they describe God's holy mountain, where God's friends will be close to him, enjoying peace and joy forever.

A Closer Look . . .

 herever you travel in the world, you will find holy places on the tops of hills and mountains. We know that God does not have a body and dwells beyond time and space. We also know that God is beyond us, our ways and thoughts, and so we think of God as "up."

Mountains and hills are signs of God's presence not simply because they are high, or "up." There's a history of people encountering God in high places. Moses met God face-to-face on Mount Sinai and received the Law there. King David conquered a mount called Zion, and there he planted the holy city of Jerusalem. When we speak and sing of Zion, we are thinking of the place in which we can reach God just as the people did in the Temple in Jerusalem. The prophets and the psalmists tell us often of Zion, or God's holy mountain, where peace will reign and a heavenly banquet will be celebrated.

People encountered Jesus on mountains, too. He preached the Beatitudes in the Sermon on the Mount. His Apostles saw him transfigured and speaking with Moses and Elijah atop a mountain. He prayed the night before his Crucifixion on the Mount of Olives. He was crucified on a hill called Golgotha. After the Resurrection, Jesus appeared to his disciples and sent them to preach the Good News. He sent them into the whole world with this mission and sent them from the place where he stood with them that day: on a mountain.

Harp

W hen we pray, we praise God for all he is and thank God for all he gives us. God's people have always praised the Lord with music. Throughout the Bible, the people of Israel speak of raising their voices in chant and melody, and they play to the Lord with instruments, including the harp. A harp is a sign of praise. It's also a symbol of David, the shepherd boy and king who praised God with beautiful music on his harp.

A Closer Look . . .

 od has given us everything that is good, starting with life itself. In return, we offer him what we can, beginning with our thanks and praise. Even if we come to God with needs and questions, we always begin our prayer with praise and gratitude.

The Bible is filled with song. After God's people crossed the Red Sea and the Egyptians were vanquished, Moses's sister Miriam led the people in a song of victory. When King David conquered Jerusalem, he danced and sang his way into the city with the ark of the covenant.

It is King David we most closely associate with music in the ancient history of God's people. As a shepherd boy, he played the harp, soothing King Saul with his music. It is said he composed many of the psalms. In the prophets and in the psalms, the people tell God that they're offering him praise, not just with their voices but also with all kinds of musical instruments, including the harp, or lyre.

When we see an image of a harp, we think not just of pretty sounds made with a musical instrument, but also of the prayers and songs of praise we offer the Lord, thankful and joyful at all he has given us and for all he is: "Give praise with blasts upon the horn, / praise him with harp and lyre" (Psalm 150:3).

Great Fish

J onah didn't want to go to Nineveh. God had called him to preach to the people there, but Jonah went the other way instead, on a boat. When a storm broke, Jonah admitted that he had disobeyed God, and, if the others thought it best, he would go overboard. Jonah was swallowed by a great fish, and he stayed inside it for three days. Then the fish spit him out, and finally, Jonah was on his way to share God's message with the people of Nineveh.

A Closer Look . . .

God created each of us, and God calls each of us, too. In the Bible we read of one person God called who tried to run the other way; his name was Jonah.

God had called Jonah to preach in Nineveh, a great ancient city. Jonah resisted God's call and boarded a boat going the opposite direction. A terrible storm came up, and the terrified crew tried to figure out whose god was angry with them. Jonah admitted it was probably his, and he suggested that they throw him overboard so the rest of the people could be spared a shipwreck.

Once in the sea, Jonah's life was preserved because he was swallowed by a great fish. He remained in that fish's belly for three days, until it spit him out. Finally, Jonah obeyed God's call. He traveled to Nineveh. He preached as God had instructed him. The result? All the people of Nineveh—even the king—repented of their sins.

The symbol of the great fish—often depicted as a whale—reminds us of Jonah the prophet. We remember that our peace is found in listening to God's voice and following him. We also remember Jesus, who followed the Father's will perfectly, suffered, died, and—after three days in the tomb—rose from the dead, which is our Good News. As God did with the people of Nineveh, he sends us a message: we can repent and live in the joy of God's love, safe from the darkness and the storms.

IN CHURCH

You are fellow citizens with the holy ones
and members of the household of God.

Ephesians 2:19

G od loves us so much that he came to earth to dwell among us. The Church is the Body of Christ on earth— still here, still loving, healing, and preaching in Jesus' name. The churches that God's people build for gathering and worship are signs to the world. They're signs that God is present and that all are welcome to come and see, to listen, and to meet the Lord.

Over the centuries, God's people have built and designed buildings with this welcome in mind. They design, shape, sculpt, paint, and build as a way of sharing the Good News through signs and symbols reaching up, reaching out, and inviting us inside.

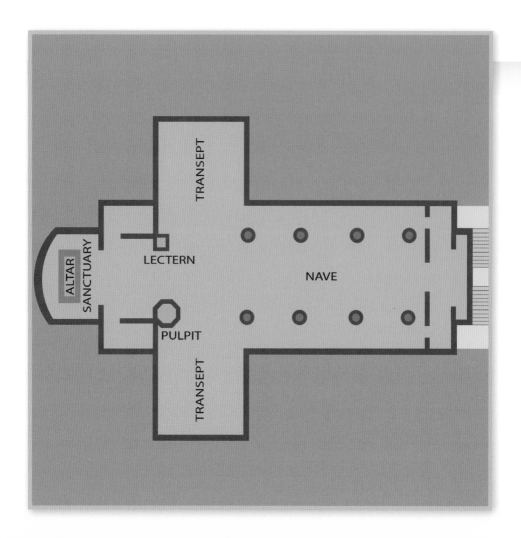

Cruciform Shape of a Church

e are the Body of Christ. When we gather for Mass, even the design of the building we're in can be a symbol of who we are. Some churches are designed to look like a cross. Not all churches are shaped like crosses, but many are, with a long part composed of a nave and a sanctuary, and arms extending from either side. As we pray, celebrate, and praise, we're being formed to be more like Jesus, inside and out.

A Closer Look . . .

LECTERN

Throughout the world and over time, Jesus' disciples gather to celebrate the Eucharist. The Mass can be celebrated anywhere, even outside. But when we love God above everything else, we want our worship to reflect how important God is to us, so we offer him our best. We want to show God how much we love him. Creating a church building full of beauty and meaning is one way we do that.

Even the shape of our churches can be symbolic. Many churches are shaped like crosses; we call this a **cruciform** design. The body of the church is called a **nave**, which comes from a word that means "ship," because the church is the ship that carries us to God. The **sanctuary** is the part of the church that holds the altar. Joining the nave and sanctuary and going across, like the arms of a cross, is the **transept**.

There are many other elements to a church's design, and not all churches are shaped like crosses. Some ancient churches, for example, were shaped like circles as symbols of heaven. But whatever the shape, the meaningful design of our church reminds us that we are not just a random group that happens to be in the same place at the same time. We are the Church, the Body of Christ, called to be like him, inside and out, visible signs of his love and grace to the world.

Cross and Crucifix

D uring the Mass, we pray, listen quietly, and sing. The priest presides. But the Mass is mostly about what Jesus does. Through the Eucharist, Jesus shares with us the grace of his sacrifice on the Cross. This is why we have a crucifix in our church. It reminds us that Jesus is with us here and now, offering himself to us in love.

A Closer Look . . .

During the first Mass, the Last Supper, Jesus took bread, broke it, and told his friends that this was his body, given up for them. Then, the next day, Jesus indeed gave up his body in sacrifice for our sins, on the Cross.

The Mass is many things. It is a celebration. It is a communion. At the heart of it all, it is a sacrifice: Jesus' sacrifice on the Cross. We call it the Holy Sacrifice of the Mass because that is what it is: during the Mass, we are mysteriously present to Jesus' sacrifice on the Cross, the mystery he shares with us then in the Eucharist. When we are present there, we are present at the greatest act of love the world has ever known, the act of love offered for you and me and for the whole world. Jesus' sacrifice brings us to God, and in it we're joined together—we are in communion.

And so, in our church or chapel where we celebrate Mass, we find a crucifix. There must be a crucifix near or on the altar for the celebration of Mass. We are forgetful and distracted—that is just part of being human—and having a crucifix always in sight during the Mass helps us keep our focus on Jesus. As we pray, sing, and praise, our hearts follow where our eyes rest: on the love of Jesus, borne on a cross for us.

Altar

When the people of Israel worshiped God, they offered sacrifices on an altar. Jesus offered a sacrifice, too: himself. To heal the world and overcome sin and death once and for all, Jesus offered his own life on the Cross as a sacrifice. At the Mass, we gather at the altar. Through the words and actions of the priest, Jesus comes to us in the bread and wine, giving the gift of himself.

A Closer Look . . .

very day in the Temple in Jerusalem, God's people offered sacrifices on altars. They slaughtered animals and brought the best of their crops. Through their sacrifices, they praised God by giving him the first and best of what they had. They also offered sacrifice as a way of atoning for sin, showing that they were sorry and wanted to change.

But the world was still broken, and sin and death still reigned. Jesus, the Word made flesh, entered the world with humility and love. He preached, healed, and gave signs of the Kingdom of God. And finally, he took the weight of our sin upon his shoulders and accepted the Cross. In the sacrifice of the Son of God, heaven and earth are brought together again, once and for all.

Jesus shares the grace of his sacrifice with us through the Eucharist, offered on an altar. An altar must be made of stone or very solid wood as a sign of Jesus, the Living Stone. An altar contains relics of martyrs, friends of Jesus who entered his sacrifice in the deepest way possible. We decorate our altar with the colors of the liturgical season, but the only other objects to be put on it are those we use for Mass: candles, sacred vessels and books, and a crucifix. This is not just any table: it's the altar of sacrifice where Jesus invites us to gather for the banquet of eternal life through him, with him, and in him.

Tabernacle

Through the words and actions of the priest, Jesus changes bread and wine into his Body and Blood during the Mass. Any of the bread—the Body of Christ—left after Communion is placed in a tabernacle. A tabernacle is a strong container that can be locked. It is kept in the sanctuary of the church or in a side chapel. A light always burns near the tabernacle, a sign of the real presence of Jesus with us here and now.

A Closer Look . . .

 hen God's people traveled through the wilderness and through the Promised Land, they carried the precious tablets of the Ten Commandments with them in a container called the ark of the covenant. Whenever they stopped, they erected a tent over the ark, a tent of meeting where God was present in a powerful way. Nearby, a flame always burned. We sometimes refer to this tent as a "tabernacle" or "dwelling place."

In our churches, a **tabernacle** is the place where the Eucharist is reserved. It must be locked, and it may be located in the sanctuary of the main church or in another chapel close by. An oil lamp or wax candle—not an electric light!—must burn nearby. That's a sign that Jesus is present. It's an invitation for us to draw near to Jesus in prayer and to take comfort that he's with us.

In the Church's history, tabernacles have been made in different shapes, all with different meanings. A tabernacle can look like a house because it's the Lord's dwelling place. It can look like a tower or a box holding a treasure. In ancient Christianity, it was common to reserve the Eucharist in a container shaped like a dove hung from the ceiling. This was a sign of the Holy Spirit, through whose power the Word of God became flesh in Mary's womb and now becomes the Bread of Life for us.

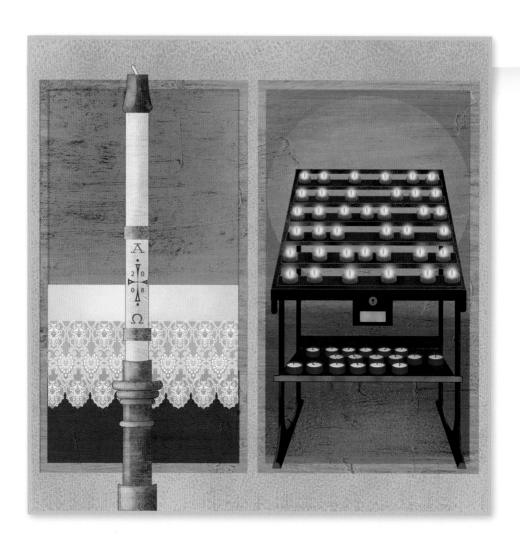

Candles

J esus is the Light of the World. He helps us see ourselves and the world clearly. Our churches are filled with candles that remind us of Jesus, the living light. During Mass, real candles must stand on the altar, and they must be lit. A large paschal candle is lit during the Easter Vigil and burns at baptisms and funerals. We light small votive candles in our churches as a sign of our own prayers, carried to God in hope.

A Closer Look . . .

There was no electricity in ancient times, so people needed candles and oil lamps. But why do we still use candles in our worship today?

Candles are symbols. They are sources of living, natural light that remind us of Jesus, the living light of the world. Candles used to be made with beeswax, and bees are important symbols for Christians. Bees work hard. They help the world by making honey and wax. So even though most candles today are made of a substance called paraffin, church candles often still have a portion of beeswax in them.

In our churches, you will always see candles on the altar. These candles are lit only during Mass. You will also see a large candle called a **paschal candle**, decorated with symbols of Jesus' Passion. This is lit for the first time from a fire at the Easter Vigil Mass. It burns during all Masses of the Easter season, and then at baptisms and funerals throughout the year.

Many churches have sets of smaller candles we call **votive candles**. We light these candles as we say a prayer. They are signs that our prayers bring us closer to the light of Jesus and that they work to bring Jesus' light to others. Because candles are consumed as they burn, these little flickering lights are also signs of what we're willing to sacrifice as we follow the Lord's will for us.

Chalice, Paten, and Other Vessels

D uring the Mass, bread and wine become the Body and Blood of Jesus Christ. We use only the most special vessels for this gift. The plate that holds the Body of Christ is called a paten. The cup that holds his Blood is a chalice. Both are made of precious metals that do not rust, decay, or break.

A Closer Look . . .

Some families have dishes they use only for holidays and other special occasions. When you bring out the good china or the Christmas plates, it's a sign that this day is not like other days.

The Mass is that kind of celebration. During that moment in time and space, Jesus himself comes among us. He brings us into the mystery of his sacrifice on the Cross, and he is present under the appearance of bread and wine.

We don't use just any cups and plates for the Body and Blood of Christ during Mass. Two vessels are used for the Body of Christ: a **paten**, which is like a plate; and a **ciborium**, which has higher sides and is more like a bowl and holds more consecrated Hosts. The cup is called a **chalice**, a word that comes from the Latin word **calix**. All these sacred vessels are to be made of precious metals for two reasons. First, we want to give God the best that we have. Second, precious metals don't decay or rust or bring contaminants into what they contain. If the entire vessel can't be made of a precious metal, at least the inside—the part that comes into contact with the Body and Blood of Christ—is.

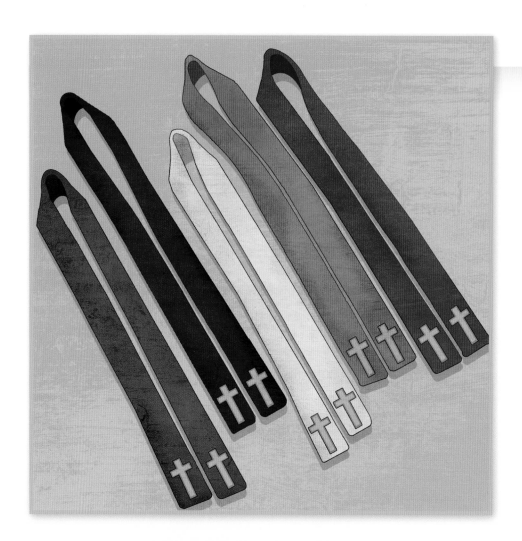

Liturgical Colors

E very time you go to Mass, you see color. The main colors you see go with the time of year. During Advent and Lent, the vestments and the cloths decorating the altar and ambo are violet, or purple. Pink is used on two special days in those seasons. During the Christmas and Easter seasons, they're white. Green is the color of Ordinary Time. On Pentecost, you'll see red, the color of the fire of the Holy Spirit, and you'll also see red on the feast days of martyrs who have shed their blood for their faith.

A Closer Look . . .

ven before you could read, you probably could recognize a stop sign by the color red. You probably knew what yellow and green meant, too.

Colors are signs to us in daily life and in our spiritual lives, too. As Christians, we are shaped by the cycle of feasts and seasons called the **liturgical year**, each with its own color. These will be the colors of the liturgical vestments, such as the stoles pictured, and the cloths that decorate the altar and other church furnishings.

Our new year begins with Advent, preparing for Christmas. Purple is Advent's color. It's a symbol of penance. Christmas is marked by white and gold. Lent is a time of deep penance and prayer, so its color is purple too, and then white and gold return for the Easter season. During both Advent and Lent, we celebrate a little break: on Gaudete (Advent) and Laetare (Lent) Sundays, we celebrate hope with the liturgical color of rose, or pink.

On Pentecost, the Holy Spirit descended in the form of fire, so red is the color of that day. Red is also the color of the feast days of martyrs, as well as of Palm Sunday and Good Friday— both days on which we remember Jesus' sacrifice on the Cross.

During Ordinary Time, you'll see green, the color of life, the reminder that when we gather at Mass, we're sharing in the gift of life, now and for eternity.

Vestments

During the Mass, the priest acts in the role of Christ, so he wears clothes that help us remember this role. He wears a white *alb* that symbolizes his Baptism; he ties the alb with a *cincture*, or rope, that is a sign of his dedication to Christ. And over that he wears a chasuble and a stole that are made in the colors of that day's liturgical feast or season.

A Closer Look . . .

e're all part of the Church, the Body of Christ, each with our own functions. During Mass, the role of ordained ministers in the Body of Christ is made visible by the clothes they wear, called vestments.

There are different styles of vestments, developed over the many centuries of the Church's life, but there are a few basics that you will see every bishop, priest, and deacon wear at any Mass you attend.

They begin with an alb. **Alb** comes from the Latin word for "white" and is a long white robe that symbolizes Baptism. A **cincture**, or rope, is tied around the alb. This is a sign of the call to be strong. A **stole** and **chasuble**, made in the colors of the day's liturgical feast or season, go next. A deacon's outer garment is called a **dalmatic** and has a different shape. The deacon's stole crosses his chest, but the priest's hangs straight down.

A bishop wears what a priest wears, plus a special large cross called a **pectoral cross**, worn near his heart. He also wears a tall hat called a **miter**, and he carries a **crozier**, or shepherd's crook, because Jesus has called him and all bishops, through Peter, to "feed my sheep."

All these vestments, in a way, "hide" the individual personality of the minister. They focus our eyes and heart on Jesus so we can listen to him as he calls each of us to our own role in his Body.

Gestures

I t's hard to hide happiness—you just have to smile! Our bodies tell the world what we feel inside. When we pray, we also talk to God with our bodies. We make the Sign of the Cross to show that we belong to Jesus. We kneel as a sign of humility. We stand to show that we are ready for the Resurrection. We fold our hands in prayer and bow our heads. We offer ourselves to the Lord, body and soul.

A Closer Look . . .

hen we are with our friends, we don't communicate with them with words alone. We hug, smile, play sports, walk together, and shake hands.

It's the same with God. God may be a purely spiritual being, but we're not. In prayer, our bodies express what is in our hearts. So, humble in God's mighty, loving presence, we fall to our knees. When it's time to listen to the Gospel with respect and express how ready we are for Jesus to come again, we stand up. We indicate that we welcome the Good News by signing our minds, lips, and hearts with the cross before we listen.

We let the world know we belong to Jesus when we make the Sign of the Cross. When we pass by the real presence of Jesus in the tabernacle, we genuflect because he's there. During the *Confiteor* at Mass, we strike our hearts as we admit our fault. We bow in awe when Jesus' birth is mentioned in the Creed. On Good Friday, we reverence the cross with a kiss, a bow, or a touch.

During Mass, the priest has his own set of prayer gestures. At the beginning of Mass, he kisses the altar. When he extends his arms in prayer, it is a reminder of Jesus on the cross.

Actions may not always speak louder than words, but in prayer, they certainly say a lot.

Stations of the Cross

J esus had to carry his cross through Jerusalem to the place called Golgotha. For many centuries, Christian pilgrims have gone to Jerusalem to walk in Jesus' footsteps. Most of us can't do that, so we do a pilgrimage right in church. Along the walls we'll find scenes of the fourteen Stations of the Cross. To help us come closer to Jesus in his suffering, we go from one station to the next, praying, singing, and meditating.

A Closer Look . . .

esus told his friends that anyone who followed him would be called to take up a cross. When we love as Jesus does, his way of sacrificial love is our way, too.

It's a way of life that Jesus showed us clearly as he carried his cross through Jerusalem to Calvary. He was unjustly condemned, was mocked, and suffered horrible pain, but he bore it all patiently out of love for us.

We follow Jesus on this way of the cross as we patiently love in our daily lives, and we pray with him along his way through Jerusalem, too.

Christian pilgrims have always liked to travel to Jerusalem to literally walk in Jesus' footsteps. Most of us can't take that journey, so we follow him in prayer. **The Stations of the Cross** that you see in a church or in other places, sometimes outdoors, help us on that journey.

There are traditionally fourteen Stations of the Cross, with the Resurrection sometimes added as the fifteenth and last station. Most of the traditional stations are based on what we read in the Bible, but others have grown from stories remembered and told from that time. We often pray the Stations of the Cross with others during Lent, but you can pray the Stations of the Cross any time. Wherever you are, you'll be walking with Jesus in love, joining your suffering to his in prayer for the whole world.

Holy Water

At the entrance to a Catholic church, we will always find a vessel containing blessed holy water. It might be in small dishes fastened to the wall near the doorways, or it might be in the large baptismal font. As we come into church, we dip our hands into holy water and make the Sign of the Cross, and we do the same as we leave. We're reminded of our Baptism and that we have been reborn as God's children.

A Closer Look . . .

ho are you? Many things: you're a young person, a member of a family, a student. Your most important identity is the one that will last forever: you're a child of God, brought into God's family through your Baptism.

Every time we enter a church, we want to remember who we are and why we're there. That's why we find holy-water fonts at the entrance of churches. These fonts might be small dishes attached to the wall by the door. Some churches have larger fonts at the entrance—it's the same fonts that are used for Baptisms.

As we enter the church, we dip our hands in that holy water and make the Sign of the Cross over our bodies. As we leave, we do the same thing. Both times, we're expressing who we are. We were baptized in holy water in the name of the Father, the Son, and the Holy Spirit. Every time we enter the church, we relive that Baptism that brought us here into the Body of Christ.

When we leave, we do the same, but this time the sign means something a little different. We're going out into the world now. We dip our hands in the waters of Baptism, we make the Sign of the Cross, and we trust that Jesus will be with us as we try to share his love in the world with courage and joy.

Church Imagery

A church building is the home where Jesus' family gathers. Like any family, we decorate our church home to remind us of who we are. In every church we'll see a crucifix and probably statues of Mary, Joseph, and other saints. The windows and paintings in the church will tell us stories from the Bible and from the lives of the saints. Everything we see in the church will have a story to tell us—and that story is ours.

A Closer Look . . .

ou're part of the Church, the Body of Christ. This Body of Christ lives all over the world, in all sorts of different places and cultures, growing in holiness every day.

It makes sense that we want the places where we are most visibly the Body of Christ—in communion with him and with each other at Mass—to be special. These buildings have different shapes and styles, some more elaborate than others. But in all Catholic churches, you will see images and symbolism.

You will see statues and paintings. These paintings will have scenes from the Bible or from the history of the Church. The sanctuary might be filled with carved or painted symbols. You'll see images in stained glass.

All of this is more than decoration. Every image in a church means something. God is greater than any of our words can capture, and symbols and images help us enter that mystery with our imaginations and creativity.

These images also remind us every time we go to Mass that the Body of Christ is more than just the people sitting in that particular building. The symbols and images of Jesus, Mary, and the saints remind us that we're part of a reality that stretches across time and space, and here in the presence of this Communion of Saints, we're with our family, and we're at home.

AT HOME

*The Word became flesh
and made his dwelling among us.*

John 1:14

W herever we are, we like to surround ourselves with reminders. We put up posters and sayings in our room that say something about us. We have pictures of family and friends, of our favorite movies, bands, and sports teams. These express who we are and who we hope to become.

More than anything else, we—young person, student, musician, athlete—are all children of God. God created us, and it's in him we find lasting peace and happiness. The signs and symbols we have in our own homes help us remember, in our busy lives, that God is always near.

Cross and Crucifix

We are Christians! Jesus' love is at the center of our life. Having a cross in our home, or even wearing one around our necks, helps us remember this. Some crosses have an image of Jesus on them. These are crucifixes. Others don't—these are just simple crosses. We can have a cross anywhere in our house so wherever we are, we remember to put Jesus first in our hearts.

A Closer Look . . .

ur days are busy and full. We study, we work, we have chores. We spend time with our friends and family; we cook, we build, we read, we celebrate, and we serve others. We want to keep Jesus at the center of our lives, but it can be hard.

Having crosses in our homes helps. There are different styles of crosses hanging in people's homes or around their necks. All of them are about Jesus and his sacrifice, but with slightly different symbolism.

First is the crucifix, which has the body of Jesus—called a **corpus**—on it. Sometimes you'll see a cross with an image of the risen Jesus on it, or at other times a plain cross without a body on it.

The Franciscan cross is a crucifix, but it is painted and colorful. It is an image of the cross from which Saint Francis heard the call to "rebuild my church." The Jerusalem cross has arms of equal length, and there's another smaller cross in each section made by the arms, symbolizing the city of Jerusalem.

The Celtic cross originated in Ireland. It's a traditional-looking cross with a circle around where the arms meet. That's a sign of eternal life.

Life is filled with good things. Keeping Jesus at the center always makes it even better, and it helps and encourages us when we look up and see a cross nearby.

Rosary

The Rosary is more than a set of beads. It's a prayer that brings us closer to Jesus through Mary. When we pray the Rosary, we pray sets of Hail Marys and Our Fathers while we meditate on mysteries from the lives of Jesus and Mary. The prayers are divided into sets of ten Hail Marys, called decades. The Rosary gets its name from the rose, a symbol of the Blessed Mother.

A Closer Look . . .

I n addition to the Mass, the most important prayer of the Church is called the Liturgy of the Hours. This is the schedule of prayers to be prayed by ordained and vowed religious men and women at certain times of the day. Over a week's time during the Liturgy of the Hours, every psalm is prayed—all 150 of them!

Long ago, people who lived outside monasteries wanted to join in this prayer practice. The tradition developed of praying 150 Hail Marys and Our Fathers—**Ave Marias** and **Pater Nosters**—in place of the psalms. This was something people could do anywhere—in their homes or out in the fields—when they heard the monastery bells ring.

The traditional, full rosary, then, has 150 beads for saying Hail Marys, with an Our Father and a Glory Be between each set of ten, called a decade. That full rosary is what we see some religious wear as part of their habit. On each decade, we meditate on a certain mystery: one of the joyful, sorrowful, glorious, or—recently added—luminous mysteries. The rosaries that most of us have are a third of that full rosary, with five decades.

This form of prayer came to be called a **Rosary**, based on the Latin **rosarius**, which means a garland or bouquet of roses, and roses are symbols of the Blessed Virgin. Praying the Rosary is like planting a garden of prayers with and for Mary.

Scapular

A s we go about daily life, God is always with us. Wearing a scapular helps us remember this. A scapular is made of two small squares of cloth, usually wool, joined by long pieces of string. One square rests on our chest, the other on our back, and it's worn under our clothes. It's a sign of faith and trust. It's a sign that we're willing to work hard as we follow Jesus.

A Closer Look . . .

Sisters, monks, friars, and other religious wear different kinds of clothes called habits. Many of these habits have something in common: a long piece of cloth that goes over their heads and hangs down to the floor in the front and in the back. This is called a **scapular**, from the Latin word for "shoulder."

Not everyone is called to religious life, of course. But sometimes people who live in the world feel a call to join themselves to the vision of a religious order. They may not be able to be a full member of the Benedictines, but Saint Benedict's way helps them draw closer to God. Laypeople who wanted to follow a religious order in the world often started to wear a small version of the order's scapular under their clothes as a sign of their commitment.

Today, many wear an even smaller type of scapular. It's two pieces of wool, usually with a picture or saying attached. The two pieces are attached with string or leather and worn under the clothes. There are many types of scapulars. The most popular is the Brown Scapular, which is associated with the Carmelite religious order.

A scapular is not a good-luck charm. It's a sign, though, that we are serious about following Jesus in a particular way. It's a sign of God's protection and of the hard work we're willing to shoulder as we respond to his call.

Candles

J esus is the Light of the World. The candles we see in church remind us of this. We can use candles in our homes, too. We can keep our baptismal candle and light it on our Baptism day. That reminds us that Jesus calls us to share his light. When we light candles that have pictures of Jesus, Mary, and the saints on them, we're bringing light into the darkness through our prayers.

A Closer Look . . .

e're not alone here on earth. We're part of a big human family living in God's creation and beyond earth, too: the saints in heaven are alive, praising the Lord. In Purgatory, souls are being cleansed and made ready to meet Jesus. What ties us all together? Prayer.

All of us are praising God together. It's not something we do only in church. We pray at home, too, and candles in our home can help our prayers.

A candle that we use in prayer is a symbol of Jesus, the light. Because candles are consumed by fire, they're also symbols of the ways we're called to let God's love consume us. That means we live for God, not for ourselves. Any kind of candle can help us remember this, but prayer candles imprinted with symbols or poured into decorated glass containers can help us even more.

These candles, with images of Jesus, Mary, and the saints, aren't magic. They're signs of the light of Jesus. They help us focus. They help us pray in the right way. We light a candle. We see the light flickering in darkness. The image of a holy person reminds us how to pray and what to pray for: to praise God with the whole Church on earth and beyond, to pray for all people, including the souls in Purgatory, and to pray for the grace to take that light outside into the world.

Patron Saints

S aints come from all parts of the world. They come from all walks of life. When we think of saints, we think of their jobs, their ministries, their families, and interesting things that happened to them. Because of who a certain saint is, he or she becomes, over time, a patron saint. That means we believe that a certain saint takes special care of people and places that have this connection with him or her.

A Closer Look . . .

 e're all brothers and sisters in the Lord, but we're all different, too. It's what makes life so interesting! The lives of the women, men, children, and young people who are canonized saints reflect this variety. Saints are all friends of Jesus, but no two are alike!

Saints come from all backgrounds. Some are wealthy, some are poor. Saints come from every corner of the earth. When we read the lives of the saints, we find queens, beggars, soldiers, children, professors, and hermits. We find people who traveled far from home and people who never left their birthplace. We find people who like to talk a lot and be around others, and we find people who prefer to be alone with God.

Whoever and wherever we are, we can find a saint who seems to match us in some way. When we say that a saint is a **patron saint**, we're saying that something about that person's life story makes him or her especially understanding of a country, a profession, a disease, or a category of people.

So we can look at the lives of the saints and find someone who we know understands us, and we might ask them for their prayers. They're our patron saint. Our patron saint might be the saint we've been named for or one whose name we'll take at Confirmation. Whoever it is, what a comfort to know we have a special, understanding friend in heaven!

Holy Cards

S aints are friends of God, and they are friends of ours. We like to have pictures of our friends, so we keep pictures of the saints, too. These pictures, called holy cards, have an image of Jesus or the saint on the front and usually a prayer on the back. We keep holy cards in our Bibles, prayer books, and other places so we'll remember that we can turn to our friends the saints for prayer anytime and anywhere.

A Closer Look . . .

The Church is bigger than our families, our parishes, our diocese, or our country. The Church is universal, and it even lives across time and space. Friends of Jesus who lived, died, and are now in heaven are part of the Church, too—that's the Communion of Saints.

There are many saints in heaven, more than we can count. We celebrate the saints known and unknown on the Feast of All Saints on November 1. There are women, men, and children who have been **canonized**, officially recognized as saints. We call upon these saints in prayer.

One way we remember saints and keep them in our daily lives is through **holy cards** and other pictures. A holy card has an image of a saint on one side and a prayer or saying on the other. We can take a holy card anywhere with us. We can keep it in our purse or wallet. We can slip it in a prayer book or Bible. We can keep a holy card next to our bed or even tape it to our wall or mirror! Wherever we take them, holy cards remind us that we are not alone. We're part of the Body of Christ, and wherever we go, these friends of Jesus can come with us, supporting us with their prayers.

Liturgical Seasons

We live in all kinds of seasons: seasons of nature, school seasons, sports seasons. Friends of Jesus live in the seasons of the Church, called liturgical seasons. We follow the liturgical seasons in Mass in church, but we can live the liturgical seasons at home, too. We light Advent candles, we say special prayers during Lent, and we decorate our homes for Christmas and Easter. We can surround ourselves with signs of Jesus' love all year round.

A Closer Look . . .

The seasons of the year shape us, inside and out. As life on earth blossoms, flourishes, and fades through the seasons year after year, we go on a journey, too. Spring, summer, fall, and winter affect how we feel and what we do.

There are other kinds of seasons too. The seasons of school: the excitement of a new year, the stress of tests and projects, the tired feelings, the satisfaction. There are sports seasons and performance seasons.

For friends of Jesus, the most important seasons of all are the seasons of the Church, or the seasons of the **liturgical year**. We know these most of all from church, but we can celebrate the liturgical year at home, too.

At home, we pray special prayers during Advent and Lent. We put up Advent wreaths and calendars and Jesse trees. We clean our homes and decorate for Christmas and Easter. We color Easter eggs. We cook certain foods for all these feasts. We give gifts, signs of God's gift of life to us. We know when our favorite saints' feast days are, and we celebrate those with stories and food. We even take out our own baptismal candles on the anniversary of our Baptisms and celebrate—because it's like another birthday!

Life on earth is beautiful. God is the reason for it all, so in all the busy seasons of life, we let our lives be shaped and led most of all by the seasons that tell the story of God's love for us.

IN THE SACRAMENTS

"I am the bread of life."

John 6:48

J esus is the Word of God. He is a sign of God's love and presence in the world. He left another sign for us on earth: his Body, the Church. The Church offers signs to the world of all kinds, most of all in the sacraments.

The sacraments are different from the other signs and symbols in this book. They are more powerful. Images and sculptures are signs and symbols because they remind us of other true things. The water, oil, bread, wine, and words of the sacraments go even further: they actually become what they signify. They are the deepest signs of all, signs that don't just remind us of God's love but also bring us into God's heart.

Water

Water gives life. Water cleans. God gives our bodies life through water. He helps our souls with water, too. We become children of God through Baptism in blessed holy water. In water, our life on earth began. In water, our heavenly life begins, too. We remember this every time we go into church and make the Sign of the Cross with holy water. We remember and thank God for giving us new life that lasts forever.

A Closer Look . . .

 ater: It's that feeling of life returning when you're really thirsty and you finally get a drink. It's that feeling of freshness after a shower or swim. It's peace, awe, and wonder when you look at the depth of the seas.

Genesis tells us that when God created, his spirit hovered over the waters. Before the rest of creation, water was here. Genesis also tells us of mighty floodwaters that covered the sinful earth and of the ark that saved Noah and his family from the waters. In Exodus, we read of the waters of the Red Sea, separated by Moses with God's power. In the history of Israel, God uses the waters of the earth to cleanse and save.

A man named Nicodemus went to talk to Jesus in the dark of night. Jesus told him that to have eternal life, he would have to be born again. How could this happen? Through water and the Spirit—through Baptism.

John had baptized people who wanted to repent of their sins and be made clean. After his Resurrection, Jesus sent the Apostles into the world to baptize in the name of the Father, the Son, and the Holy Spirit. This was the Baptism he'd told Nicodemus about. It is the Baptism that cleanses us from sins. We're reborn through these baptismal waters, reborn as children of God to live with God forever as we continue to respond to the grace he gives us.

Oil

O live oil is smooth and shiny, and it smells good. People in
biblical times not only cooked with olive oil but also put it
on their wounds and used it to clean their bodies. Priests,
prophets, and kings were anointed with oil as a sign that God
had chosen them. God chooses us, too, so we are anointed
with holy oil, called Chrism. We are anointed with Chrism at our
Baptisms and Confirmations.

A Closer Look . . .

live trees are gnarly, with dusty green leaves, and they can live and produce fruit for a long time. Olives have been important since ancient times, not just as food but also because of the oil that the pressed fruit produces. Ancient peoples cooked with olive oil. They used it to clean their bodies. Olive oil was used to help wounds heal and to make hair and beards shine.

Anointing with oil was also a sign of being chosen. Kings like David and Solomon were anointed, and so were priests and prophets.

God still calls us to follow him, and we are still anointed. We use a special blessed oil, called **Chrism**, fragrant with incense, in sacraments as a sign of that call. This Chrism is used to anoint during Baptism and Confirmation. Chrism anoints a priest's palms when he is ordained and a bishop's head when he is consecrated. The altar of a new church is anointed with Chrism.

There are two other kinds of oils used in sacraments. The oil of catechumens is used to anoint people on their journey to becoming Catholic. The oil of the sick is used to anoint people in the Sacrament of the Anointing of the Sick. All these oils are blessed in the cathedral during Holy Week and then kept in a special place in your parish church, signs that God is strengthening us, as he did his people long ago, to serve him.

Bread

Our bodies need food to live, and so we eat bread. Our souls need food, too, and so Jesus gives us himself, the Bread of Life. At the Last Supper, Jesus took bread, broke it, and gave it to his friends. He told them that the bread was his body now. When we go to Mass, we're there at the Last Supper again. We need Jesus to bring life to us, and he does. He's the Bread of Life, shared with us so we can live fully on earth and forever in heaven.

A Closer Look . . .

 hen God created our first parents, he gave them all the food they would need in the garden. When God's people wandered in the desert, seeking the Promised Land, he gave them bread from heaven, called manna.

God created you and me to serve him in this world and to be happy forever with him in the next, and he gives us the food we need for that journey, food for both body and soul.

Jesus said that he is the Bread of Life, and that if you want to live forever, you have to eat of his flesh. This was hard for some people to believe, so they stopped listening to him. But the Apostles stayed. They stayed through the Last Supper, when Jesus did give his very self to eat under the appearance of bread. They continued to share that Bread of Life and passed it on to us.

The bread Jesus used was unleavened, without yeast, so that is what we use at Mass. The individual pieces of the bread are called **hosts**, which comes from the Latin word for "sacrificial victim." Jesus told us that a grain of wheat must die in order to sprout and give life. Jesus gives his life to the world and then shares that life with us, so we can die to our selfishness and live.

Wine

Grapes grow in big, full bunches. These bunches hang from vines in a place called a vineyard. For ancient people, grapes were a symbol of a good harvest. Grapes produce wine, a sign of blessing and celebration. Jesus told parables about vineyards. He said that he is like a vine who gives life to us, the branches. And at the Last Supper, Jesus took a cup and told his friends that this wine would now be his blood, shed for them and the forgiveness of sins.

A Closer Look . . .

 hen Jesus spoke about vines and vineyards—which he did often—his listeners understood. Grapes and the wine made from them were important in daily life. Wine—not juice or milk or soda—was an important everyday drink, as well as a sign of celebration. When people heard Jesus speak of grapevines, vineyards, and wine, they understood.

Jesus told parables about workers in vineyards. When people heard this, they remembered that in the past, the prophets had spoken of God's work in the world as something like a vineyard: growing and flourishing, created by God but nurtured through our labor too.

Jesus also compared himself to a vine. He said that he was the vine and that his friends were branches. We can have life only when we stay connected to the vine. If we're cut off, we die.

At the Last Supper, Jesus shared food and drink with his friends: bread and wine. It is traditional to have several cups of blessing at a Passover, or seder, meal. Jesus took one of these cups of wine, blessed it, and told his disciples that this was now his blood, the blood of the new covenant, shed for us and for the forgiveness of sins. That's the cup we share at Mass.

Grapes are gifts from God that can change into something new: wine. Jesus changes wine and makes something new: his blood, his life, so we can be changed too.

Words

hen Jesus was on earth, he spoke words. He preached, he taught, and he told parables. When Jesus worked miracles, he spoke. He told people they were healed and forgiven. He called to fishermen, "Follow me." The Church is Jesus' Body on earth today. In sacraments, Jesus still speaks. In the Sacrament of Reconciliation, we hear Jesus' words of forgiveness. In the Sacrament of Matrimony, two people speak words of promise to each other and to God.

A Closer Look . . .

 od said: "Let there be light." The Book of Genesis tells us that God spoke creation into being. Words express who we are. In creation, God's word comes to life. The universe reflects God's mind.

Jesus is the Word made flesh, dwelling among us. When he walked on earth, he—the Son of God—spoke. He revealed himself. He taught people about God's love. Through his words, he shared mercy, forgiveness, and healing. Through his words, he shared himself.

The Church is the Body of Christ on earth today. Through the Church, Jesus acts and speaks in the world, especially through the sacraments. Jesus meets us through the signs and symbols of sacraments. Every sacrament has its own liturgy—its own words. Through these words, Jesus speaks now, to you and me.

In Baptism, through water and words, Jesus calls us to him and forgives us. In Confirmation, through words and laying on of hands, we receive the Holy Spirit. In the Sacrament of Reconciliation, we hear Jesus' words of forgiveness. In the Sacrament of Holy Orders, through words and laying on of hands, Jesus calls people into ministry. In the Sacrament of the Anointing of the Sick, through words and anointing, Jesus heals. In the Sacrament of Matrimony, through words, a man and a woman join their bodies and souls as one, with God's grace. In the Eucharist, through Jesus' words spoken by the priest, bread and wine are changed into his Body and Blood. Through words, we meet the Word.

Hands

hen the people of Israel wanted to show that God was sharing his power with a human being, they used their hands. They extended hands in blessing. They laid hands on a person's head. Jesus touched people when he healed and blessed them. The Apostles laid hands on someone as a sign of the Holy Spirit's presence. During Confirmation and ordination, the laying of hands on a person's head is a sign of the Holy Spirit.

A Closer Look . . .

e wave, we clap, we create. Through our hands, we give signs, and we bring change.

God works through our hands, too. He works every day, as—with our hands—we share the gifts he's given us. But just as Jesus was present through the work of his hands when he walked on earth, he's present today through the work of our hands in the sacraments and other actions of the Body of Christ.

With our hands, we make the Sign of the Cross. The priest holds his hand out in blessing as he speaks Jesus' words of forgiveness to us. During Mass, the priest extends his hands over the bread and wine as he speaks the words of Consecration.

"God's right hand" is a symbolic way we think of God's authority. When the Israelites laid hands on a person's head, that was a sign that God's Spirit and authority were with them.

For the Apostles, the laying on of hands was a sign of the Holy Spirit's presence (Acts 8:17). When a man is ordained a priest, the bishop lays hands on his head. And when we celebrate the Sacrament of Confirmation, we are anointed with Chrism (oil), and the bishop or priest lays his hands on our head. Through these hands, God gives us his Holy Spirit, and now it's time to share that love and grace with our own hands.

Almighty and eternal God,

it does not displease you

that images of your saints are carved or painted.

For when we look at these images with our eyes,

    we are reminded

of their holiness and friendship with you.

We ask you to bless these images and sacramentals,

made in honor of your friends,

    bearing signs and symbols that point us to you.

We pray that when we see these images,

    we will think of your love and mercy

and seek to be witnesses to that love

    in our own lives.

Bless and sanctify this image, made

    in honor of your saints.

Grant that, as we pray in the presence of this image,

    we will be drawn closer to you,

now and forever, through Jesus Christ, our Lord.

Amen.

— Adapted from Solemn Blessing
of an Image, *Rituale Romanum.*

About the Author

Amy Welborn is the author of *Loyola Kids Book of Saints*, *Loyola Kids Book of Heroes*, *Loyola Kids Book of Bible Stories*, and more than twenty other books for Catholic children, teens, and adults. A former catechetical leader, she has a passion for inspiring children to understand their faith at a deeper level and for helping them live their faith with confidence and joy.

Visit her website at **www.amywelborn.com**.